"Marc Lesser's skill in developing ways to make modern workplaces meaningful and compassionate, as well as productive, keeps getting better and better. His aptness in finding just the right phrase that will stay with you (helped, in this case, by Homer Simpson, the Buddha, and Alice in Wonderland) is prodigious. His wisdom about the ways we commonly work against ourselves is tempered by his gentleness. In *Finding Clarity*, his fifth book, Marc shows us how clarity, compassion, and accountability not only can but must go together for organizational and personal success. The book is full of clear and actionable practices for developing these skills. Thanks, Marc, for a lifetime of reenvisioning what it means to go to work."

— **Norman Fischer**, poet and Zen Buddhist priest, author of *When You Greet Me I Bow: Notes and Reflections from a Life in Zen* and *Selected Poems 1980–2013*

"This important book gives the fortunate reader a clear path to the cultivation of clarity in relation to moral integrity and accountability."

— **Rev. Joan Jiko Halifax**, abbot at Upaya Zen Center

"Because he is a highly trained Zen teacher, Marc Lesser resembles an expert fly-fisherman. He is mindful of the backcast, allowing the line to unfurl before committing to a forward flick to settle the nearly weightless fly in a beguiling manner onto water, where the prize resides. The fly is insight itself; the line is mindfulness, having both feet planted in the stream; and the artistry to describe it is his training and gift. Without cant or jargon, this book offers the reader every tool they need to be more productive, efficient, and happy. And, like every good fly-fishing instructor, Marc helps them learn the patience and skill to unwrap the occasional snarls and tangles that accompany the joys of being alive. Don't miss this book."

— **Peter Coyote**, actor, author, Zen Buddhist teacher

"In clear and direct terms, *Finding Clarity* offers the reader powerful tools for integrating a flexible, effective, and compassionate approach to living and leading in today's world. The author, Marc Lesser, draws from his extensive experience as a business leader, Zen teacher, and executive coach to bring two powerful ideas — accountability and compassion — together not as opposing concepts but as central components for vibrant relationships and leadership in any context. Any leader of a team or organization, any parent or friend, or anyone with a relationship where being present, accountable, and available is important — which is all of us — will find this book extremely practical, actionable, and impactful toward being the best possible version of themselves."

— **Rich Fernandez**, CEO of Search Inside Yourself Global

"Marc Lesser has a unique ability to combine unlikely concepts from his 'stealth Zen practice' and make them accessible to read, practice, and integrate into daily life. I so appreciate this book in its wisdom and ease and highly recommend it to all leadership teams."

— **Susan Griffin-Black**, founder and co-CEO of EO Products

"Marc Lesser is an extremely insightful leader, writer, and Zen teacher. *Finding Clarity* is a remarkably helpful and hopeful book for anyone seeking greater well-being and impact, better relationships at work and at home, and a clear sense of their path forward."

— **Deb Nelson**, founder and executive director
of the Just Economy Institute

"This book is a straightforward, easy-to-understand guide for how to take action and responsibility in our relationships and work environments in a caring yet courageous way. A refreshing perspective that's much needed in today's world."
— **Dr. Kristin Neff**, associate professor at University of Texas at Austin and author of *Fierce Self-Compassion*

"Marc Lesser is someone who embodies his message. *Finding Clarity* is a clear, thoughtful, generous book. Written in an engaging, accessible style, it is both wise and down-to-earth. It helps us get to the heart of communication as well as put heart in communication. Marc teaches us how to transform conflicts and breakdowns into opportunities for alignment and true teamwork. In these times of misinformation and divisiveness this book is an invaluable guide to greater understanding and productive harmony. Highly recommended!"
— **James Baraz**, coauthor of *Awakening Joy: 10 Steps to Happiness* and cofounding teacher at Spirit Rock Meditation Center

"This kind of clarity is hard to find, never mind cultivate within an organization, and so it is priceless. Anybody who puts mindfulness and the ancient 'wisdom beyond wisdom' practices of the Heart Sutra at the heart of their work deserves the deepest respect and attention. The invitation and the challenge then is, critically, implementation — that is, to actually live it, to do nothing less than to embody and enact it within one's own life and the culture of one's organization. No one has more cred and more experience in this regard than Marc Lesser. Paying attention to Marc's approach may not only transform your business; it may literally transform your life."
— **Jon Kabat-Zinn**, founder of MBSR (mindfulness-based stress reduction) and author of *Full Catastrophe Living* and *Coming to Our Senses*

"In *Finding Clarity*, Marc Lesser shares his vast experience as a leader, a Zen practitioner, and a human finding his way through this world. This book offers an array of practices that support change in our work, our lives, and the world."
— **Sharon Salzberg**, author of *Lovingkindness* and *Real Life*

"*Finding Clarity* offers us what we need most right now — the practical tools to create cultures and relationships that integrate grace and accountability. In addition to personal wellness, this is the path to organizational performance. I loved Marc Lesser's earlier book *Less*, and this will be my new favorite book to give to friends and colleagues I care about."
— **Jay Coen Gilbert**, cofounder of B Lab

"Marc Lesser has done it again, integrating the depth of Zen practice with immediately useful business skills. Written with humor and grace, *Finding Clarity* shows us many practical ways to bring heart into expecting — and getting — important results from others...and oneself. And he shows how to bring responsibility and strength into our friendships and even romantic relationships. I'm imagining a world in which more people bring compassion and accountability together, and it's a really good one!"
— **Rick Hanson, PhD**, author of *Resilient: How to Grow an Unshakable Core of Calm, Strength, and Happiness*

FINDING CLARITY

Also by Marc Lesser

Seven Practices of a Mindful Leader:
Lessons from Google and a Zen Monastery Kitchen

Know Yourself, Forget Yourself: Five Truths to Transform
Your Work, Relationships, and Everyday Life

Less: Accomplishing More by Doing Less

Z.B.A. — Zen of Business Administration:
How Zen Practice Can Transform Your Work and Your Life

FINDING CLARITY

HOW COMPASSIONATE ACCOUNTABILITY
BUILDS VIBRANT RELATIONSHIPS,
THRIVING WORKPLACES,
AND MEANINGFUL LIVES

MARC LESSER

New World Library
Novato, California

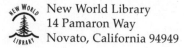

New World Library
14 Pamaron Way
Novato, California 94949

Text design by Tona Pearce Myers

Library of Congress Cataloging-in-Publication Data

Names: Lesser, Marc, date, author.
Title: Finding clarity : how compassionate accountability builds
    vibrant relationships, thriving workplaces, and meaningful lives
    / Marc Lesser.
Description: Novato, California : New World Library, [2023] |
    Includes bibliographical references. | Summary: "A ground-
    breaking path to professional communication and success that
    melds essential concepts previously considered incompatible:
    compassion and accountability"-- Provided by publisher.
Identifiers: LCCN 2022059252 (print) | LCCN 2022059253 (ebook)
    | ISBN 9781608688333 | ISBN 9781608688340 (epub)
Subjects: LCSH: Communication--Religious aspects--Buddhism.
    | Work--Psychological aspects.
Classification: LCC BQ4570.C586 L475 2023 (print) | LCC BQ4570.
    C586 (ebook) | DDC 294.3/3--dc23/eng/20221215
LC record available at https://lccn.loc.gov/2022059252
LC ebook record available at https://lccn.loc.gov/2022059253

First printing, April 2023
ISBN 978-1-60868-833-3
Ebook ISBN 978-1-60868-834-0
Printed in Canada on 100% postconsumer-waste recycled paper

10   9   8   7   6   5   4   3   2   1

*Will you ever bring a better gift for the world
than the breathing respect that you carry
wherever you go right now? Are you waiting
for time to show you some better thoughts?*

— WILLIAM STAFFORD

Contents

Preface

I had to live this book in order to write it. As a long-term mindfulness practitioner and entrepreneur with an MBA degree, I sometimes describe myself as a stealth Zen teacher working in the business world.

I've discovered that as we engage with the continual challenges and possibilities of our daily lives, our work, and our world, we uncover a trio of universal needs: a clear mind, an open heart, and integrity in our dealings with others. Achieving these is not always easy, but increasing our self-awareness and interpersonal skills is how we live with more depth, compassion, and effectiveness. My life's work has been to engage with these life-changing practices and to convey them in accessible and actionable ways in the workplace and in all aspects of our lives.

My professional experience is wide-ranging: For ten years I lived at the San Francisco Zen Center, including a one-year stint as the director of Tassajara Zen Mountain Center; I received an MBA degree from New York University Business School; and I founded and was CEO of three companies, including Search Inside Yourself Leadership

Institute, a company launched inside of Google's headquarters. I currently train executives, employees, and businesses in fostering mindful leadership toward creating highly effective and supportive teams and cultures. Looking back, I can see how this journey began when I was growing up in a small suburban town in central New Jersey.

As I child, I could feel the tension inside my home and in the world outside. My father had been in the army during World War II, serving on the front lines in France and Germany. After he returned, he was diagnosed as being manic-depressive. I imagine he also suffered from post-traumatic stress. My mother was often consumed with the pain of my father's condition and her inability to help him.

I walked every day through a small cemetery to and from elementary school, examining carefully the gravestones, noticing the birth and death dates, with a sense of wonder. At school we regularly practiced "duck and cover," holding our heads underneath our desks in case the Russians dropped nuclear bombs. I had a strong urge to understand and help my father as well as a growing sense of despair about our world.

At the same time, much of my day-to-day life was spent playing sports. I was particularly fond of bowling, baseball, and golf. I dreamed of becoming a professional bowler when I was thirteen and a professional golfer at age sixteen. In high school I was captain of my wrestling team. Sports provided a respite from the confusion of family and the outside world, and at the same time, it was an important venue for exploring my sense of self and the power of working together toward a shared purpose.

When I was a college freshman, my life began to take

a very different shape. I had always wanted to understand how the mind works, but this concern came into the forefront in this new environment. I discovered a wide range of people and friendships in my dormitory and on campus, and I developed a passion for reading and learning. I was particularly drawn to literature and humanistic psychology, existentialism and Zen. A professor guided me in experimenting with hallucinogens as a process for better understanding myself and to widen my perspective of what is real and what really matters. With this combination of people, study, experiences, and drugs, my mind and my heart opened. Strong feelings and new possibilities and aspirations emerged. With these openings, I felt severely limited being in school, and I wanted to explore the world outside of college and outside of New Jersey.

I decided to take a one-year leave of absence from Rutgers and go to San Francisco to enroll in a program that included meditation and classes in Eastern and Western psychology and spirituality. During that time, I visited the San Francisco Zen Center. I was immediately drawn to the physical practice of meditation and to the Zen tradition, which is deep, simple, surprising, and steeped in both seriousness and a sense of humor. A subtle but clear voice said, "This place is worth ten years of my life." That decade, during the most formative years from my early twenties to my early thirties, was life-changing.

In addition to intensive daily meditation practice and study, one of the more surprising lessons was the importance of work as a core part of Zen practice. I took on a variety of leadership roles, and during my tenth year in residence, I was asked to be director of Tassajara Zen Mountain

Center, the first Zen monastery in the Western world, located deep in the Ventana Wilderness in central California. I was surprised how much I enjoyed leadership. I also discovered the impact of leadership for creating heartfelt and thriving work cultures that produce great results. I wondered why everyone wasn't integrating mindfulness and leadership practices. While I knew I had a good deal of learning and growing to do, I felt a tremendous sense of possibility in the integration of these disciplines, and I decided this would be my life's work.

After I left the Zen Center, I spent two years at New York University Stern School of Business, where I earned my MBA degree. Then I launched my first company, Brush Dance, one of the first companies in the world to make products from recycled paper. During my fifteen years as CEO, I put into practice my ideas about integrating mindfulness in the workplace. This involved a lot of trial and error, but the results spoke for themselves: Brush Dance became a very successful, multimillion-dollar company, selling innovative, inspirational products around the world. Then one day, one of my mentors said to me, "It's time for you to leave this small publishing company. You have much larger things to do with your life."

"Like what?" I asked. For months, I had also been feeling like it was time for me to leave, but I was afraid to walk away from my "child." I also wasn't sure what to do next.

"This you will have to discover," she responded.

When my board became aware of my ambivalence, they asked me to leave, which made my exit from Brush Dance bumpy and stressful. No one likes being fired from a company they began, even if this has happened to some business greats, like Steve Jobs. It was painful and not how I wanted to transition from the company I had founded and led for nearly fifteen years.

Two years later, in 2006, I discovered that next "larger thing" my mentor had urged me to seek when I received a call from a Google engineer asking if I was interested in creating a mindful leadership program inside of Google. Of course, I said yes, and at Google, I immediately saw how my rich experience in the monastery and in Zen practice and my experience having led a company for many years could come together in useful and important ways. This merging of disciplines defined the Search Inside Yourself program we created, which helped Google employees — from executives to engineers to kitchen staff — develop healthy relationships and environments in their workplace and in any situation. During the five years of teaching mindful leadership through this program, I saw a genuine hunger to improve listening, to work more skillfully with conflicts, to be more authentic, and to connect with others more deeply.

Emerging from this work at Google, I cofounded and was CEO of the Search Inside Yourself Leadership Institute. For another five years, I had the great opportunity to lead a company from an idea to a thriving enterprise, as well as teach mindful leadership around the world to diverse audiences, ranging from government intelligence agencies to the Girl Scouts of America, from enormous corporations like Microsoft and SAP to small nonprofits. After that, I developed my own coaching and consulting practice, which is what I do today.

In every setting, I have noticed that two core issues

arise again and again: finding clarity and developing what I have come to call compassionate accountability. Whether at work or at home, people want to identify a clear vision of success, which includes both achieving specific results and fostering a positive, supportive culture. They want more skill working within teams or as a group to solve problems in ways that create alignment and connection, not divisions and conflicts. Over time, the twin competencies of finding clarity and compassionate accountability have become essential to my leadership coaching and to helping others create healthy and effective group environments.

How This Book Will Benefit You

This book, which summarizes the work I've developed throughout my life, is a primer in the art and practice of finding clarity through compassionate accountability. I present the core tools and practices for opening your mind and heart and developing more aligned and healthy relationships and cultures. Any joint effort and important relationship requires these skills, and I've written this book so that it speaks to issues in the workplace, in families, and in relationships. It is for leaders, managers, employees, and contractors in any kind of business. Even in a one-person business, entrepreneurs must work effectively with vendors, accountants, and of course customers — who always demand and require accountability. This book is for people in any kind of group, committee, team, club, or civic organization. It is for families, but perhaps particularly parents and children.

The practices can also be applied to any kind of challenging situation we might find ourselves in: from dealing with "bad" drivers on the highway to resolving family conflicts, from building a cooperative, effective team to managing team members who aren't "pulling their weight" — so that everyone remains dedicated to their shared goals. These are also essential practices for effectively engaging with the climate crisis and creating a more safe and just world. Finding clarity and compassionate accountability provide a path for developing more understanding and alignment, preventing or healing unhealthy conflicts, and working skillfully and effectively with different perspectives.

Ultimately, this book is a guide to finding more depth, flexibility, and effectiveness at work and in your everyday life through cultivating greater freedom — greater emotional freedom, freedom from conditioning and mistaken beliefs, and freedom to choose how to respond in the most caring and effective ways. Finding clarity and compassionate accountability are the essential practices for living a meaningful life and helping to solve our most essential problems.

Introduction

How Our Thoughts, Feelings, and Actions Create, and Can Change, Reality

We live in uncertain, complex, troubled times. We always have, though there is compelling evidence that we are living in one of the least-violent times in history; modern medicine has vastly improved our overall health and longevity; and tremendous progress has been made toward reducing hunger, poverty, inequality, and many other social ills. So why does it always feel like life today is not just hard but maybe harder than it's ever been?

One reason is because change itself, good or bad, can be surprisingly disruptive, and our world now changes constantly and at a blistering pace. To take one obvious example, technology has improved our lives in countless ways, but it's also disrupted entire industries, along with our workplaces, schools, families, and relationships. Smartphones have changed how we communicate and interact, how we connect with the world and one another, and yet for every positive benefit, there's a corresponding loss. We connect more easily and widely but not as deeply. We have access to endless information, but as a society, we can't seem to agree about what is meaningful, important, or even true.

In addition, comparing ourselves to previous times rarely makes us feel better. Despite the many areas of human progress, we still face dire, existential, and even unprecedented threats: nuclear war, climate change, pandemic diseases, terrorism, racism, authoritarian leaders, and on and on. Better or not, the modern world is often dangerous and precarious and our future uncertain.

I feel we are at a crucial tipping point in our workplaces, our families, our society, and our planet. There is a tremendous need to find clarity: in our thinking, feelings, goals, actions, relationships, and results. To solve problems, to be effective and successful, to lead a more satisfying life, we need to see problems clearly and foster agreement on what they are. We need to identify a shared vision that guides our efforts to fix things or achieve what we want. With this clarity, we have the potential to create warmer, more caring, more focused, and more effective workplaces and relationships, as well as to help heal social rifts and even repair our world.

To me, clarity begins with acknowledging and embodying that the world is not always what it seems. A tree, on one level, is just a tree, and it can be dissected and explained in biological terms. Yet when looked at from the perspective of a larger reality, a tree is a complete mystery. We don't really know what it is or how it got here. The same is true of everything, including us, we humans here on Earth. Birth, life, death, blood, hearts and hands, stone and sky, consciousness — all are mysteries, sacred mysteries to behold with wonder and awe.

Clarity means seeing the world from both perspectives:

the ordinary and everyday, where a tree is just a tree, and the mysterious, which means acknowledging the unknown source of reality. Living with this awareness creates something of a paradox. In ordinary reality, we face many dualities — of life and death, you and me, accepting what is and seeking change, being confident yet humble — and these dualities are important for living our ordinary lives. They can provide clarity in our everyday, relative world. But clarity in the larger reality means seeing beyond or outside of these dualistic, relative ways of perception. On this level, clarity dissolves distinctions.

That said, in everyday terms, I think clarity is embodied by the following attributes. It is:

- transparent
- easily heard
- easily visible
- unbiased, or not fooled by greed, aversion, or ambiguity
- not limited by dualities (or includes multiple perspectives)
- free from entanglement

However, finding clarity and living with more clarity for ourselves is only the first step. We also need to work cooperatively to take effective action and solve the crucial problems facing us. What I've found is that the key to this is fostering more accountability as well as more compassion. The concept and practice of compassionate accountability combines two essential attributes that are often mistakenly treated as separate and unrelated, if not incompatible. In fact, the opposite is true.

Accountability is about more than simply living up to our obligations and responsibilities. It means devoting ourselves to seeing clearly and aligning around facts. It means practicing skillful truth-telling. Rather than turning away from conflict, or practicing avoidance, it means working with conflict and destructive emotions to resolve them. Accountability means dedicating ourselves to connecting and aligning with one another for the benefit of all and working toward a shared vision of possibility, transformation, and success.

That said, accountability can easily foster harshness, judgment, blame, and division if it is not balanced by care and compassion. In working toward accountability, it's more effective and more sustainable to approach one another with empathy, kindness, and a genuine desire for understanding. That means listening openly, being flexible and forgiving, seeking to help and support others, and believing that *how* we solve problems is as important as *what* we do to solve them. Finding clarity within ourselves and working effectively and compassionately with others may be the most important and urgent work facing us right now.

That is my hope for this book — that it will teach the related arts of finding clarity and fostering compassionate accountability. This means aligning around a vision of success and transforming the inevitable conflicts and breakdowns into possibilities. This means learning to see and act with more genuine care, integrity, and effectiveness at work and in all our important relationships. This means creating healthy, vibrant relationships and environments that skillfully foster alignment and trust, which are essential to accomplishing any goal.

Avoiding Conflicts Is Trouble

A lot of troubles boil down to avoidance. When we avoid problems or cover over conflicts, and act as though everything is fine when we know it's not, this can lead to even bigger problems. Equally important and just as problematic, however, is not having a clear vision of what we want in the first place. If we don't have a clear vision of our desired results in mind, it almost inevitably creates confusion and conflict. This is particularly an issue in groups. As a business consultant, I'm always surprised at how often leaders and managers don't articulate what success looks like for their teams or *how* they aspire to work together. Then they are surprised when employees don't work well together, develop negative or uncooperative attitudes, and to protect themselves, tend to pass the buck, avoid conflict, and ignore problems.

The consequences of a lack of a clear vision and of problem avoidance are painful, and they undermine workplace relationships and company cultures as well as family dynamics and interpersonal relationships.

In my executive coaching practice, I work with CEOs and leaders from a wide range of industries — including Google, Roche, Microsoft, California Academy of Sciences, San Francisco International Airport, and Beneficial State Bank, to name a few. Working toward alignment, not only around outcomes and process but also around conflicting motivations, is consistently a primary issue. Nearly all my most important meetings and interventions address issues of avoidance, of unclear goals, of conflicts and competing motivations, and of negative feelings and judgment.

In companies, I often hear these statements:

"He only hears what is working and shuts out whatever is not working."

"She only sees what's lacking, and not all that I've achieved."

"My supervisor continues saying yes to taking on more work, even though we are totally overloaded and stressed."

"There is too much on my plate and not enough resources."

"She just doesn't listen."

"He just doesn't care or take responsibility."

"I don't feel valued."

"My manager doesn't understand me."

"We are working hard, and she wants us to do even more."

"I don't feel safe expressing my doubts."

Each of these statements can be amended to apply to families, parenting, or any important relationship. Here are some statements I hear from parents:

"I just can't seem to get through to my son."

"When I ask my daughter how she's doing, all I get is 'fine.'"

People in core relationships often say the following:

"My husband just doesn't understand and never asks."

"My girlfriend and I seem to be growing apart."

Accountability, and the Lack Thereof

To one degree or another, resolving these issues often comes down to two things: becoming more accountable and acting with more compassion, both with others and with ourselves. That said, accountability is not a very popular topic. When hearing the term *compassionate accountability*, my publisher's first response was, "You know, most people don't like accountability."

No, they don't. But why? I think it's because accountability tends to be preceded by the phrase "lack of." As in, we are quick to notice a lack of accountability in others — in the form of broken commitments, breached expectations, and plain bad behavior — while hoping to avoid being held accountable for our own errors, mistakes, and misjudgments. The prime example is the dreaded performance review, where the boss evaluates how we're doing, and after a few perfunctory pats on the back (if we're lucky), they point out all the ways we aren't measuring up and need to do better. Ouch.

Accountability, or a lack of accountability, is a major issue in society in general. Much press and commentary are devoted to holding (or not holding) politicians, celebrities, CEOs, and other public figures accountable for their misdeeds. In the corporate world, mention the word *accountability*, and people often think of the collapse of Enron, AIG, or Lehman Brothers, not to mention Uber, Theranos, and WeWork. There are endless examples of breaches of trust, truth, and transparency and of a radical lack of accountability.

Accountability and well-being in the workplace are

major concerns. It is estimated that managers spend 25 percent of their time resolving workplace conflicts, most of which involve issues of accountability — from misunderstandings and lack of alignment around goals to disruptive bad behavior. Here are some research statistics:

- In a recent survey, Gallup found that only 20 percent of all people are thriving at work, 62 percent are indifferent on the job, and 18 percent are miserable.
- From 2020 to 2021, employee engagement declined in the United States from 36 percent to 34 percent.
- US employees spend approximately 2.8 hours each week involved in conflict. In total, this means US employers are paying around $359 billion to their employees to focus on conflict instead of on productive work.
- In the United States, 60 percent of employees don't receive conflict management classes or conflict resolution training.
- On average, companies with a healthy corporate culture report a turnover rate of 13.9 percent; companies with a poor culture report a 48.4 percent turnover rate.
- A 2021 UK study reported that 485,800 UK employees resign each year due to conflict on the job, and it costs UK employers approximately £2.6 billion (at publication about $3.16 billion in US dollars) each year to replace those employees.

In our families, on average, 27 percent of family members are not speaking with each other, and 40 percent of family members have been in serious conflict at some time. Typically, people have little or no training about how to resolve conflicts within families and friendships. The idea of "visions of health" in family life is almost completely absent.

Sometimes, when we look at the state of the world and political leadership, both in the United States and worldwide, we can start to wonder if anyone will ever be held accountable for anything. Society can't even seem to agree on the same facts, whether regarding the role of government or individual rights. Whether the issue is women's rights, racism, police violence, or our climate emergency, no one wants to be held responsible and everyone is pointing fingers.

Accountability Matters

Poet David Whyte was once leading a public reading when he was approached by a man who, in an abrupt and direct American way, said, "We have to hire you."

David responded in his dryly, slightly suspicious Irish-English fashion, "For what?"

The man paused, then responded: "The language we have in the corporate world is far too small for the territory of relationship and collaboration we've entered."

"That was an intriguing invitation," David later reminisced. "A poet's work is all about creating a language big enough to represent both the world you inhabit and the next, larger world that awaits you."

The man was a senior leader at Boeing, the head of strategic planning. David Whyte's poetic and uplifting approach became an integral part of the work of a major manufacturer of commercial airplanes, shifting the company toward a more heartfelt way of working together.

Why did an airplane manufacturer value this? Today, it takes as many as six thousand suppliers to build a modern airplane. There are six million parts on one 747, and forty thousand rivets on each wing. Over the forty-three days it takes to build a jumbo jet, workers fill in a bar chart each time one of fourteen thousand individual jobs is completed. A single plane may be tagged with as many as a thousand rejection slips before it is finished — that's a thousand gaps between the plan and vision and the reality, each gap needing accountability, needing to be addressed and aligned, to build a flying machine that you and I and our loved ones can count on, not only to get us to our destinations but to keep us safe and alive.

The level of collaboration and accountability required in building a plane, or almost anything, and in the vast majority of our workplaces — not to mention the complexity of our daily lives — is staggering. However, the effectiveness and innovation of collaboration benefits tremendously from something larger, equally important, and not always visible: the human spirit of genuine care and love for the work, as well as the heartfelt connection of working and accomplishing together. The Boeing executive was pointing to the powerful blend of alignment and accountability, integrated with the human heart, which is the essence of compassion. He wanted his company to practice working together with open minds and open hearts. This led to Boeing being regarded, according to the *Guardian*, as "the gold standard of American industry, bringing international travel to the world and getting NASA to the moon by upholding a rigorous degree of excellence on the factory floor."

When this isn't the case, it can lead to disaster, and Boeing is also an example of what can go wrong. In 2018 and 2019, two Boeing 737 MAX airplanes crashed, resulting in the deaths of 346 passengers. The 2022 documentary *Downfall: The Case Against Boeing* investigated these tragedies and found not only that Boeing knew beforehand about the mechanical flaws that led to the crashes, but that to avoid losing money, executives allowed the planes to keep flying as they tried to fix the problem. The film's director, Rory Kennedy, concluded:

> There were many decades when Boeing did extraordinary things by focusing on excellence and safety and ingenuity. Those three virtues were seen as the key to profit. It could work, and beautifully. And then they were taken over by a group that decided Wall Street was the end-all, be-all. There needs to be a balance in play, so you have to elect representatives that hold the companies responsible for the public interest, rather than just lining their own pocketbooks.

In 2021 Boeing was fined $2.5 billion by the US Justice Department after being charged with fraud and conspiracy in connection with the two crashes. Investigators alleged that Boeing employees, including a pilot, misled air-safety regulators about how the MAX's flight-control system worked.

Of course, no practices or processes will prevent every accident or every miscalculation. Great cultures can shift with new people and new attitudes — shifting away from compassion and accountability and becoming overly focused on profits. At the same time, risk is inherent in all decision-making. The question is how to maximize the results we want and reduce risks by leveraging a process that includes aligning not only around objectives and processes but around the deeper streams of emotions, awareness, motivations, and social skills.

What Makes Compassionate Accountability Different

In theory, we all want and value accountability. This is what makes us so surprised, disappointed, and angry when it's missing, when there is a lack of it. We know it's necessary. When accountability is present, not only does it help prevent terrible decisions, breakdowns, and bad behavior, but it fosters other positive attributes: more alignment, trust, and understanding. Even when people and organizations have varied, sometimes competing perspectives, when they are accountable to one another and work passionately and wholeheartedly toward shared goals and visions, amazing results can be achieved. Working together with care and alignment can feel great and foster tremendous personal and professional development. There is great beauty in being part of a team, a family, or a group of friends when we operate like a talented jazz ensemble, taking cues from one another, learning from one another, and creating magnificent music together.

Accountability can be defined as an acceptance of responsibility for honest and ethical conduct in our words and actions. It's the process of aligning our differences through greater understanding, and it's the ability to see and experience from multiple perspectives.

Accountability may be one of the most important skills and practices for human beings, especially during this time of dynamic change, formidable threats, and significant possibilities. Accountability is particularly essential in our workplaces, where people engage and interact closely in an array of relationships and across a multitude of teams. Within dynamic cultures aspiring to get things done, accountability helps us to find solutions and overcome obstacles with creativity and to work with a sense of urgency. Accountability is also an essential practice at the heart of all our relationships: in our families, our centers of education, and across our political landscape.

Accountability alone, though, is not enough. By itself, it can be cold and harsh and can undermine the very visions and goals we aim to achieve. Humans need more than aligning around goals. We breathe, act, and live in relationship to one another. We need to care about each other. We need to feel safe and connected to those we work with. And we need meaning, motivation, and purpose — a sense that our work, our goals and visions, and our relationships matter. Without care, trust, connection, and purpose, we risk feeling unsafe and threatened by those who would "hold us accountable," and so slip into conflict avoidance.

An integral part of accountability is holding each other accountable not only for what we are achieving but for how we are working together, for the quality of our relationships.

Any business needs to value what it produces along with its most important asset: people.

The word *compassion* literally means "to suffer together." It means to access our own human vulnerability, as well as our common humanity. Among emotion researchers, it is defined as the feeling that arises when we are confronted with another's suffering and feel motivated to relieve that suffering.

> An integral part of accountability is holding each other accountable not only for what we are achieving but for how we are working together, for the quality of our relationships.

Compassionate accountability integrates care, connection, and love with clarity, alignment, and purposeful action. It is a trainable method to leverage trust and understanding to achieve greater effectiveness and results, to reduce misunderstandings and conflicts, and to provide a way to more effectively achieve our goals, objectives, and visions. Cultures that emphasize compassion without accountability tend to be low in energy and ineffective. Those that emphasize accountability without compassion can be cold and often are harsh. Environments that are low in both compassion and accountability are dull and chaotic. The sweet spot, the place for cultivating healthy, thriving, effective cultures, is an environment that excels in both compassion and accountability: the practice of compassionate accountability.

	LOW COMPASSION	HIGH COMPASSION
LOW ACCOUNTABILITY	Dull and chaotic	Low-energy and ineffective
HIGH ACCOUNTABILITY	Cold and harsh	Caring and effective

This book provides an approach or a set of skills for fostering compassionate accountability, which is both a method for working with others and a way of being. It helps us avoid unhealthy conflicts, align and work with different viewpoints and perspectives, and create paths for working skillfully and effectively with the inevitable obstacles, errors, mistakes, and conflicts that arise.

As David Whyte and the Boeing executive recognized, compassionate accountability is exactly the kind of language we need today: in our business world, in our families, in society and politics. It's the language of the heart, of care and love, integrated with the language of honesty, integrity, and effectiveness. It's the language of problem solving, of focusing on gaps, needs, and misunderstandings, while applying the healing properties of understanding. Our enormous challenge and opportunity is to transform the ways we work and live together to take care of one another while achieving results that matter.

Clarity, Compassion, and Accountability

Tamban-kan is a Japanese expression that means "a person who carries a board on their shoulder." This describes someone who understands things from a limited perspective, a person who holds tightly to a particular view. It could describe someone who sees themselves as a failure while ignoring their successes and dismissing the miracle of being alive. It could describe someone who thinks they are *only* an ordinary human leading an ordinary life with nothing remarkable to offer others or the world.

At some point, maybe often, we are all a *tamban-kan*. So

in every situation, our aim should be to remove the board we carry on our shoulder so we can see, feel, and experience that we are also holy, sacred, connected to the cosmos, and with vast abilities, including the ability to shape and influence our shared reality.

Finding clarity is a path open to all humans, regardless of our backgrounds or identities. When we remove the board from our shoulder, a world of possibilities opens — the possibility of living fully both in this ordinary world and in the world of depth and sacredness, the world of our heart.

I intend the practices in this book to be a guide or a path for integrating the ordinary and the sacred in our lives. They are practices of clarity, accountability, and compassion — of responsibility and alignment, a search for facts and truths, with care and love. The benefits of this work are many:

- It's a path of self-development, self-understanding, and emotional and spiritual growth. We learn about ourselves through our relationships.
- It's a way of deepening our relationships and cultivating greater connection. So often we skim the surface of our relationships to protect ourselves or because we lack the skills or courage to risk more.
- It leads to a more effective workplace. It helps align actions with results by fostering greater trust, innovation, and collaboration.
- It's a path toward creating a shared vision and learning and growing together.
- It is a core part of creating great cultures — ones

that are highly caring and highly focused on results.

- It helps heal rifts, divisions, and conflicts in our families and important relationships by integrating caring and love with integrity and openness.

My Approach: A Summary

To summarize what I explore more fully in this book, here is a cheat sheet for finding clarity and practicing compassionate accountability:

Start by stopping: Knowing and understanding ourselves takes time and effort, but it is so worth it! Stopping, really stopping — such as through a regular meditation or reflection practice — is like hitting the reset button. With each inhale, we notice our thoughts, our stories, our emotions, fears, and desires, and we become familiar with our patterns. Then with every exhale, we let go of everything, including our ideas of right and wrong, of good and bad, and our ideas of who we are as well as our self-help plans for others. To find clarity, start by stopping.

Turn toward inner conflicts: Engaging with our inner conflicts is an important part of growth and development. We all contain many parts — success and failure, optimism and pessimism, introversion and extroversion. Facing, not avoiding, inner conflicts helps us appreciate our own depth, complexity, and flexibility. Understanding our paradoxes and contradictions is the path to clarity and freedom.

Engage with outer conflicts with compassion: Tangles, conflicts, and misunderstandings with others provide opportunities for growth, learning, and intimacy. We can notice any tendencies to avoid conflict, and instead lean in. Listen. Be curious. Experiment with ways to address conflict, and practice self-compassion.

Strive toward alignment via accountability: Accountability helps us align our actions with our goals. This means holding ourselves and others accountable for our expectations and choices, for the process, and for how we respect and take care of our relationships.

Cultivate courage: By letting go of and transforming desires and fears and avoidance patterns, we cultivate courage.

Prioritize relationships: Compassionate accountability is a practice of cultivating connection, understanding, trust, and real intimacy. The apparent goal is to accomplish important things together, but at heart, it's about fostering healthy, vibrant, and effective relationships.

Build supportive communities: At its best, this work builds healthy communities that can accommodate and support everyone to achieve shared goals. This expresses itself differently in different contexts: at work, in families, among friends, on sports teams, in therapeutic environments, and so on. Being part of a community not only feels good, but it is a tremendous way to learn and cultivate listening, understanding, and alignment — even in the midst of inevitable challenges, misalignments, and breakdowns.

Practice! It's all practice: In stillness and in movement, at work and at home, every moment provides an opportunity to learn, to grow, to understand. Work, family, and relationships are terrific cauldrons for cultivating self-awareness and insight. Everything in our lives is practice.

Expect change to happen quickly and gradually: When it comes to inner and outer growth, it helps to be both patient and impatient. On the one hand, we can't expect instant results. Lasting change requires patience and diligence. On the other hand, don't wait. The moment is now. By continually seeking change, we allow for it to unfold in sudden and surprising ways.

Small Changes Lead to Enormous Results

When I teach meditation to Google engineers, one question I'm often asked is, "What is the least amount of time I can meditate and have it make a difference?"

These are not lazy people. Many are driven to succeed and have been almost since birth. This is really an engineering question about leverage: What is the least amount of effort I can expend that will result in the most change? It's the same question that Archimedes, the great mathematician and physicist of early history, explored in his proof of the principle of the lever. As he famously proclaimed, "Give me a lever long enough and a fulcrum on which to place it, and I shall move the world."

I usually respond to the Google engineers, "One breath. One breath with the full awareness of breathing, and letting go of who you think you are, can make an enormous difference in your life."

The fulcrum of human development is how we approach changing our limiting and mistaken beliefs and shifting our identity. If we shift one small misunderstanding about ourselves, our identity and even our whole world might shift. We might change from "someone who writes" to being "a writer," from "someone who is impatient" to "a good listener." Shifting our identity, our own view of ourselves, is where we gain the most leverage for transforming greed, aversion, and pain into possibility, acceptance, and satisfaction. In a moment, we can shift from someone who considers themselves stuck or "a failure" to someone who is learning and discovering. Bringing awareness to our patterns, not only through our thinking but through the physical, body-engaged practice of breath and meditation, is a tremendous way to create leverage for change in our identity and behavior.

Solutio is what medieval alchemists called the process of making something more fluid, so it is more workable and able to be transformed. When a problem is difficult, we describe it as "hard." When it's been transformed, we say it's been "solved." One breath, one insight, one small shift can be like applying WD-40 to the places in our thinking and in our hearts that have hardened.

Another question that arises when I'm doing this work — particularly with individuals, teams, and company cultures — is whether change primarily occurs through specific insights and important "aha" moments or happens gradually over time through ongoing hard work and practice. Of course, as I write above, my response is yes: Change occurs both suddenly and gradually. Zen teacher Shunryu Suzuki often compared the rate of change as being like walking in the midst of fog. You hardly notice anything happening until at some point you are surprised to find you are wet.

The practices of finding clarity and of compassionate accountability require us to be both confident and humble, so that we move forward with courage but without necessarily knowing all the answers ahead of time. My advice as you read this book echoes what the Buddha was fond of saying: Test these concepts, tools, and practices, and see how they work for you.

It takes confidence to grow and to learn, especially in the realm of emotions, identity, and behavioral change. It requires humility to be a student, to try new things, to make mistakes. It takes courage to admit what we don't know. A good dose of awe and wonder, combined with a growth mindset and the courage to explore, may be our most important tools.

> A good dose of awe and wonder, combined with a growth mindset and the courage to explore, may be our most important tools.

Sometimes what appears difficult or impossible may be exactly what is most needed. Compassion and accountability can often seem to be opposed, but by combining them, we have the power to change everything — how we see ourselves and how we engage in our work, our relationships, and our life. Finding clarity and compassionate accountability just might be what are needed most in our workplaces, our leadership, our families, our politics, and for our planet.

1

Be Curious, Not Furious

Once we believe in ourselves, we can risk curiosity, wonder, spontaneous delight, or any experience that reveals the human spirit.

— E. E. Cummings

"We are descendants of the nervous apes," my Google scientist friend Mario often says to me. "Our ancestors that were chill were killed. The ones that were regularly scanning for threats survived. We have inherited their genes."

We are extremely adept at scanning for threats, especially at work where the stakes are high. There are threats to our competency, our status, our autonomy, and our livelihoods. When threatened, our emotional alarm bells go into full alert mode, and we easily shift from alert to a full display of anger. The antidote to scanning for threats and responding with anger is to train ourselves to be curious about our feelings and the intentions of others. What conclusions do we make and what stories do we tell when we get even the slightest whiff of a threat? I sometimes think we should all have these four words — "be curious, not furious" — sewn into our clothing for easy and regular access so we learn to pause and question.

When I was a child, I had a grade-school teacher who often admonished me whenever I inquired about issues she either didn't understand, didn't want to reveal, or was just too tired to respond to: "Curiosity killed the cat." This was her constant warning to my young and inquiring mind. Her message was that I needed to protect myself from what I didn't know. Staying safe meant not asking. Or as some put it today, I needed to "stay in my lane."

Apparently, the expression "curiosity killed the cat" was first used in 1598 in a play where William Shakespeare was one of the actors. The original phrase said either "care" or "sorrow" killed the cat, but over the years and through translations, *care* and *sorrow* morphed into *curiosity*. How unfortunate. More times than not, I suspect that curiosity is what saves cats.

Curiosity comes naturally. It's how we learn and grow. And curiosity may be the most powerful and important attribute for cultivating clarity, fostering compassionate accountability, and finding more effective solutions to our problems.

As an executive coach, I often work with leaders and managers who feel stuck, frustrated, or both. They make statements like:

"Nothing ever changes in my organization."
"I feel depleted, sometimes furious after our team
    meetings."

"I don't feel acknowledged in my work for who I am and what I do."

In many workplaces, cynicism, lack of wholeheartedness, and disengagement often seem to be everyone's default attitude. One reason is because creating relationships and cultures of trust requires ongoing vulnerability, skill, and curiosity. I've noticed that if we are not cultivating trust, we are cultivating cynicism, and putting genuine effort into cultivating trust is hard work.

When we don't feel heard or recognized, when we don't see changes implemented and problems solved, cynicism comes easily. Curiosity is a potent antidote for this. It's the first step for creating trust and cultivating environments where we bring our whole selves to our work, family, and relationships. Curiosity helps us to be fully engaged with others.

Homer, Buddha, and Alice Walk into a Bar...

In practice, what does it mean to be curious? What are we meant to be curious about, and how does this help us find clarity and develop compassionate accountability? To help answer these important questions, I decided to consult with three esteemed experts: Homer Simpson, the Buddha, and Alice in Wonderland.

Homer Simpson: Accountability Expert

Homer Simpson is a well-known expert on suffering and self-pity. He exemplifies a profound lack of agency. Nothing ever goes right for him, and whenever something does work out, that seems to happen only so that he might fail later in an even more spectacular fashion. Perpetually self-involved, Homer is particularly proficient at seeing himself as a victim of circumstances and at evading accountability.

Not that Homer ever gives up. He is continually hopeful that this time things will go his way. He has high expectations even though his every effort seems to be met with painful obstacles, challenging conflicts, and uncooperative people. When he is yet again frustrated by events, Homer's famous lament is, "Why does everything have to be so HARD!?"

I find myself echoing Homer fairly often these days. I have come to label this particular reaction as "my inner Homer," though it could be called "my inner grump" or "my inner victim."

Relationships, especially in the workplace, can be challenging. Conflicts, differences of perspectives, and downright bad behavior crop up, sometimes when we least expect it. Relationships require our care and attention, and at times immense skill, in order to more fully understand ourselves, our emotional lives, our patterns, and the many ways we are fooled by our own assumptions and mistaken beliefs. It takes effort to understand others and to work more effectively with conflicts. Changing and the possibility of transforming our relationships and our environments requires both inner work and outer work. It means altering our views about ourselves and how we see the world; it means growing our communication skills and how we work with misunderstandings and breakdowns.

This endeavor frequently has us wondering, along with

Homer: Why *does* everything have to be so hard? To better understand that, let's turn to our next expert.

The Buddha: Clarity Expert

The Buddha has been revered for more than two thousand years for his efforts to transform suffering into satisfaction and greater freedom. His story starts in the Indian Himalayas, where a king and queen had a son, a prince, whom they wanted to be happy. So they provided him with all the support and material goods they could and completely sheltered him from the outside world. Had this been Homer Simpson, the story might have ended there. But over the years, the prince grew bored, unsatisfied, and restless with the endless comforts of his life, and with the help of one of the palace servants, he managed to escape one night so he could see how the rest of the world lived.

He was surprised and transformed by what he saw. He came across a person who was sick, a person who was old, and a person who was dying. He was deeply moved and upset by how much difficulty, pain, and struggle people experienced. He was also curious. He wanted to understand the source of suffering and to discover a way to effectively engage with the questions of birth, life, and death. After a series of trial-and-error experiments, he decided to explore being still.

Legend has it that he spent forty-nine days sitting in silence under a fig tree, which became known as the Tree of Awakening. The young prince had a series of profound insights, during the course of which he developed himself into a fully free and awakened being — someone who was no longer tossed around by desires and fears. Unlike Homer, the Buddha turned inward and located the true source of suffering: not our external condition, but our inner one. He vowed to devote the remaining years of his life to teaching others why they suffer and how to transform this suffering into greater satisfaction and freedom.

The Buddha found an answer to our eternal question, Why is everything so difficult? It's simple: Life becomes difficult when we grasp for what we want and push away what we don't want in unhealthy ways. We become confused and frustrated by our greed and aversion.

The story of the historical Buddha is all of our stories. It's the story of leaving our comfortable worlds, our known environments, and becoming more aware and more mature. It's the story of the human search to find what matters most, to find our true homes, our internal homes: This lives in our hearts and minds, and it influences our way of being, or how we live and work with others. It's a path of finding our place in the world, which is about helping to make the world a better place, as best we can. It's also the story of seeing challenges, conflicts, difficulties, impermanence, and pain, not as something to avoid, but as an integral part of the path to learning and growing. It's the story of how attempting to shelter ourselves from pain and difficulty doesn't work.

The Buddha's Path for Transforming Pain

After he was finished sitting under the Tree of Awakening, one of the Buddha's first teachings was a set of insights and practices known as the Four Noble Truths. These are four key lessons for how to live with greater clarity, compassion, and accountability:

The first lesson: There is no way to avoid difficulty, sickness, and suffering. There is no avoiding conflict. We are all born and we all die. If we are lucky, we will reach old age, with all its limitations and diminishments.

The second lesson: Suffering and frustration are caused by being attached to desires and avoiding or pushing away what we don't want. So much of our suffering is caused by the push-pull of greed and avoidance: We pursue what we like or need while denying what we don't like. The ensuing messiness, breakdowns, conflicts, confusions, and misalignments that result affect all our relationships.

The third lesson: With curiosity, and the self-awareness of the true source of suffering, happiness and satisfaction are possible. Genuine freedom is possible: freedom to love ourselves and to help others. Happiness comes through engaging with and shifting our relationship with our desires and our patterns of avoidance. We still strive for what we need and want, we build families and help our friends, but we let go of unhealthy, mistaken, limiting beliefs and misguided expectations. We work to accept whatever happens, while aiming for positive changes.

The fourth lesson: The path to freedom is to live a life of integrity — to not be fooled by or pushed around by our desires and aversions. To live more in reality rather than through the lens of greed and fear. The path to freedom is to realize that everything is a gift that has been given to us.

• • •

Humans bring a multitude of desires and aversions into nearly everything we do, including our own identities and especially how we experience and relate to others. According to the Buddha, greed, hatred, and delusion come with the human package. They are part of our evolution. We all have an inner Homer.

The Buddha's teaching is the core of finding clarity — that through our attention and practice, we can transform our mistaken beliefs. We can find skillful and effective ways to work with our desires and aversions.

How? For this, let's turn to our third expert.

Alice in Wonderland: Curiosity Expert

In Lewis Carroll's novel *Alice in Wonderland*, at a critical point in her journey, Alice is surprised and amazed at how quickly and continuously she and her surroundings change. At one point, she stops and looks around at how different things have become and blurts out: "Curiouser and curiouser!"

Curiosity is the starting point for finding clarity and for putting compassionate accountability into practice. Alice goes on to ask herself: "Who am I?"

Then she answers her own question: "Ah, that's the great puzzle."

Alice's curiosity is not only aimed at the external world and events but shines the light of curiosity inward, right to the heart of the matter of self and personal identity. This is exactly what the Buddha did: turned his gaze inward.

Two underlying problems that our three experts struggle with are contending with change and our sense of identity. Our ability to work and live within the dynamic constancy of change greatly influences how we manage our expectations of ourselves and our relationships. Our sense of identity — the way in which we experience ourselves, our core values, and our way of being in the world — greatly impacts and influences how we work, play, live, and interact with others.

So if Homer represents the universal problem of expressing the anxiety and frustration of being human, and Buddha represents the solution, Alice names the method for achieving it: curiosity. This is the unconventional source of creative solutions to our most pressing problems. And the practice that these three figures represent together is summarized by this chapter's title: Be curious, not furious. When things go wrong, don't be shocked or get mad; accept that this will happen and be inquisitive. You and the world are not what they seem. Being furious cuts us off from being open, from exploring, and from learning and growing. Curiosity is the essential practice.

Difficult People

"What's the best way to work with difficult people?"

This is one of the most common questions I hear while leading mindful leadership trainings inside of companies or during public leadership workshops. Whenever I'm asked this question, I become curious. Very curious.

I like to make eye contact with the person asking the question to try to see if the person is aware that they, too, are at times one of those "difficult people." The question itself can be a subtle form of taking on the role of a victim, since it implies that the person might be blind to how they

themselves can be negatively perceived by others. By labeling certain people or behaviors as "difficult," the question
is making a judgment, and it echoes our "inner Homer"
tendency to not want to be held accountable for our own
role in "difficult" relationships.

Sometimes I even ask the person directly, "Are you, at
times, one of those difficult people?"

An important and fundamental distinction to make is
between "difficult people" and behaviors or actions that we
find difficult. This particular pattern, of labeling difficult
behavior as a kind of "character flaw," is so pervasive that
it has a name: attribution error. This refers to how, when
someone does something that hurts or angers us, we tend
to judge that person's entire character. They become, in our
minds, that label. And once we label them a "difficult person," all their actions fit under that umbrella. I suppose,
from an evolutionary perspective, this is an effective process of protecting ourselves and defending our tribe from
those "others" who pose a threat — that is, those with specific unwanted "character flaws."

A strange and rather pervasive human behavior pattern
is that we tend to judge others by the impact their actions
have on us. We judge ourselves by our intentions.

This process — from feeling the impact of another person's behavior on us to drawing conclusions and assigning
labels — happens quickly, often outside our conscious thinking or choice. Not only does it apply to individuals, attribution error can quickly and easily expand to much larger
groups. Within companies, sales groups can form judgments
about the operations team; customer service groups can
judge marketing teams. Staff employees can judge leadership

teams, and leaders can judge staff. In our
wider world, we label someone who
changes lanes without signaling a
"bad driver," someone who arrives
late to the office a "lazy employee,"
someone who cuts in line at the
store a "rude person," and so on.
For a variety of reasons, people can
label whole categories of "others" —
white people and Black people, Democrats
and Republicans, Jews and Muslims — as angry, ungrateful,
stupid, untrustworthy, dangerous, and on and on, all based
on profoundly powerful attribution errors.

> A strange and rather pervasive human behavior pattern is that we tend to judge others by the impact their actions have on us. We judge ourselves by our intentions.

Often the process begins with an underlying belief or
judgment that we've heard from those we work with or
grew up with. At times it begins with feeling hurt, uneasy,
or threatened — a simple "ouch." Someone says something
or does something and we respond by feeling hurt, angry,
put down, or not seen. This reaction can arise with how
someone looks at us.

The practice of finding more clarity within ourselves
and employing compassionate accountability begins with
becoming more curious about these reactions and why they
have arisen. Skillfully engaging in the practice "be curious,
not furious" means to feel and act with a sense of greater
safety, instead of scanning for threats. It means to feel more
satisfied instead of focusing on what is lacking or needed.
It means to feel and act with a greater sense of connection,
not disconnection. It also means developing effective strategies for working more skillfully with strong emotions,
which the rest of this chapter focuses on.

Fostering Safety and Satisfaction

We humans have evolved for two distinct purposes: (1) to stay alive and (2) to pass on our genes. Period. An extremely effective way to stay alive is to constantly scan for threats. But while this helps keep us alive, it's also stressful and leads to a variety of problems, both with our own well-being and in our relationships. It means that we tend to assume the worst in others. It also means that we easily see others as threats.

Additionally, this tendency of scanning for threats leads to a strong inner critic. We are often scanning for threats internally, asking: *Am I safe, am I okay, what did I do wrong, what might go wrong?* Again, this is an effective strategy for staying safe and staying alive, but it's not so good for seeing our world with more clarity.

Practicing Safety

With practice, we can counteract this tendency to scan, externally and internally, for threats. While scanning for threats comes naturally, we can train ourselves to be able to feel safe. A great practice, during quiet times or throughout the day, is to ask yourself: *What does it feel like, in my body, to be safe?* Then, notice when you are scanning for threats and let that reaction go. When you notice yourself making judgments about yourself or others, about good or bad, right or wrong, imagine that, in this moment right now, you are

During meditation practice, or throughout your day, ask yourself: *What does it feel like, in my body, to be satisfied, to not need or want anything?*

safe, completely safe. Simply experiment with letting go and see what happens.

Of course, there are situations when we are not safe, and some threats require urgent action. Fortunately, we humans have developed a well-honed radar for discerning safe from genuinely unsafe situations. If the house is on fire, that is not the time to practice curiosity. Either put the fire out or get out. For the large majority of "difficult" situations in our daily lives, however, immediate action isn't necessary. Instead of instantly responding to an email that makes us angry — or to a child who speaks in a tone we don't like — we can notice that our threat alert has gone off, be curious about why, and do whatever we need to feel more safe and less threatened, allowing us to respond appropriately to the situation.

Practicing Satisfaction

We humans have also evolved to be dissatisfied. From an evolutionary perspective, this is important. After a meal or after sex, our satisfaction is short-lived, which prompts us to eat or have sex again, both to improve our quality of life and to further our species. Dissatisfaction is our default mode no matter what we bring our attention to — our clothes, entertainment, our job, our spouse. We always want more and better. Again, from an evolutionary perspective, this is great, but it's not so good for our well-being or our relationships.

During meditation practice, or throughout your day, ask yourself: *What does it feel like, in my body, to be satisfied, to not need or want anything?* What if right now you have everything you need? During meetings at work, or at the dinner table, experiment with being curious about what is actually needed. Do you need a second piece of pie? If you feel hurt, put down, or ignored by someone, do you need to respond with anger?

The Stretch Zone:
Becoming Comfortable with Discomfort

Like Homer, we all want to be comfortable, but being curious means having the courage to step outside of our comfort zone. In practice, what that entails varies, but overall, it means asking new questions, trying new things, and being open to seeing the world differently. However, it's also possible to try to change too much or too fast. The sweet spot of curiosity and learning is what I call the "stretch zone." This is the place where we are stretched outside of our usual patterns and known world just enough so we can learn, explore, grow, and change. But if we go too far, we can enter the "panic zone," where we feel anxious and begin to shut down.

The "Stretch Zone Chart" on the next page shows what this looks like. In essence, keep this dynamic in mind as you try the practices in this book, such as finding safety and finding satisfaction. If you notice that taking a risk is exciting and challenging, then you are in the stretch zone. But if trying something new causes intense anxiety, a sense of overwhelm, or lost sleep, recognize that you've slipped into the panic zone and adjust until you feel less anxious and more confident.

Recognizing the Panic Zone

A good example of someone who found himself stuck in the panic zone is Morris, the chief operating officer (COO)

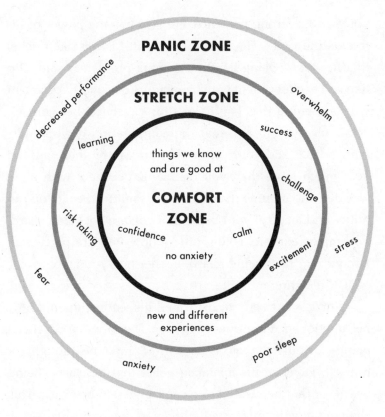

Figure 1. Stretch Zone Chart

of a midsize manufacturing company. Morris was often perceived as aggressive and at times angry. He sometimes would get into conflicts and take inflexible positions. His colleagues found him difficult to work with. People who reported to him sometimes felt unseen or at times attacked.

In one of our meetings, I was struck when Morris told me that he was afraid of not being heard. *Wow*, I thought to myself, *the gap between how he experiences himself and how others experience him can be as wide as the Grand Canyon.*

You see, Morris is six-foot-two, well-built, with a deep

voice and a strong presence. He also has the power of his role as the COO. His view of himself, his mistaken belief that he wasn't being heard, was a big problem. I said, "I'd like you to experiment with being more curious. Experiment with assuming that you have a big presence. Let yourself acknowledge and feel that the combination of your role, your power, and your physicality are felt by those around you, much more than you realize. Experiment with more wonder, and assume that your words matter. See if you can notice and let go of your belief that you are not being heard. You might explore asking others how you are perceived. Are you, in fact, being heard, even when you are curious, gentle, listening more?"

Morris's curiosity transformed his leadership and how he functioned within his company. The more he practiced being curious, the more he shifted how he thought of himself. He shed his mistaken belief that he wasn't being heard, or that he needed to be aggressive to be heard. This changed how he interacted with everyone in his life.

It can be really challenging to see clearly and be curious when the stakes are high and our amygdala, the brain's alarm bell, is ringing off the charts. Our emotions are turned upside down. This can happen when we feel judged, criticized, or put down in public, such as in a meeting. We might lose it when we receive a particularly challenging email or when our teenage daughter walks into the house at 1 a.m. when she agreed to be home by 11 p.m.

These are important times to be curious, not furious, in order to try to see more clearly.

Working with Difficult Emotions

You are in a meeting, sitting around a conference table with the company CEO and seven members of your leadership team, reviewing the results of a recent important project. One of your colleagues, Sarah, who is ten years older than you, makes a comment about what you and your team have not yet accomplished. You feel that Sarah is judging you unfairly. She is criticizing you and your team and distorting your efforts. You feel your chest tighten and anger rising; your blood begins to boil. What to do?

In a 2005 study, psychologists Kevin Ochsner and James Gross explore three primary strategies for working skillfully with difficult emotions: attention, reframing, and acceptance (see figure below).

Figure 2. Emotional Management Strategies

The first strategy, shifting your attention, is relatively easy to do, but it has the least amount of sustainability and learning. The second, reframing your experience, is somewhat more challenging and more sustainable than shifting your attention, and it's less challenging and sustainable than acceptance. The third strategy, acceptance, is the "emotional Jedi" strategy. It's the most difficult and the most sustainable, and it leverages emotional change and learning.

1. Shifting Attention

This is the practice of shifting our attention as a way of not being thrown into reacting when we feel hurt or angry.

Practice: When a strong feeling of anger arises, bring your attention to your breath. Or practice with a physical movement, such as opening and closing one of your hands.

2. Reframing the Situation

Reframing is a way of using our cognitive ability to see our situation differently. Seeing through another, perhaps comedic lens can help. When we feel hurt or angry, we can experiment with being more curious about the facts of the situation and explore other interpretations.

Practice: When a strong feeling arises, try to see yourself and the situation from another person's perspective or from multiple perspectives. Consider what positive motivations or intentions others might have. Or find some humor in the situation.

3. Accepting Discomfort

By accepting discomfort, we can transform pain into possibility. This is the "Jedi" way of working with difficult emotions.

Practice: Let yourself feel the pain and discomfort fully, and find your own sense of acceptance and openness. One image to explore is the practice of "meshing." Imagine your body to be like a screen mesh. Let challenging emotions in, acknowledge and feel them, and let them go through your body.

• • •

I spend a lot of my time teaching these self-awareness practices and ways for expanding our worlds and for working with difficult emotions. When I'm being hard on myself or feeling frustrated, when my own "inner Homer" emerges, I try to say to myself: *How curious. Isn't that interesting! I'm doing that thing that I teach others not to do.* Just this acknowledgment, a tiny dose of curiosity, goes a long way toward shifting my feelings, my state of mind, and what I do next.

2

Drop the Story

Ever since the Cognitive Revolution, Sapiens have thus been living in a dual reality. On the one hand, the objective reality of rivers, trees, and lions; and on the other hand, the imagined reality of gods, nations, and corporations. As time went by, the imagined reality became ever more powerful, so that today the very survival of rivers, trees, and lions depends on the grace of imagined entities such as the United States and Google.

— Yuval Noah Harari

My mother was once a finalist for a one-million-dollar prize in the New Jersey Lottery. She had grown up in a working-class family and had been a secretary for most of her adult life. My father accompanied her for this major event. He also grew up in a family that struggled financially. He dropped out of graduate school to fight during World War II and then worked as an electrician following the war.

My parents, and the ten other lottery finalists, were invited to Shea Stadium in New York for the announcement of the winner and the runners-up. This lottery had the potential to make a major difference in my parents' financial lives. The etymology for the word *lottery* happens to be "fate."

As the numbers were drawn, my mother excitedly held the official lottery ticket in her hand. When she heard her number announced over the stadium loudspeaker, she leaped out of her seat with excitement. As a runner-up, she had just won ten thousand dollars, but my father sat in his chair, glum and depressed over not winning the million-dollar first prize. He looked at my mother and said, "We will always be losers."

One event; two completely different, conflicting stories. My mother's most beneficent good luck was my father's unfortunate fate. As Yuval Noah Harari points out: There is the reality of ten thousand dollars and the imagined reality of what that means.

Facts and What We Make of Them

A profound human truth is that there are events and there are our interpretations of those events — or the stories we tell ourselves about those events. Some find a long commute horribly frustrating, while others use that time to plan or relax. Some welcome rain and others curse it. Some approach a company off-site as an exciting opportunity to foster connections with colleagues while others regard it as a waste of time and resources that interrupts their productivity. Every conversation, every action, every email, every meeting — one event, multiple interpretations.

Or put another way: Any event is both objective and subjective. There are the facts of what happened and the conclusions we draw. We are always interpreting our experiences, and those stories are real and powerful. In fact, we can't help weaving stories, but part of finding clarity and acting with compassionate accountability is learning when and how to "drop the story." This practice involves developing self-awareness of the stories we tell ourselves and evaluating how well, or how badly, they are serving us. Then, whenever we recognize that a certain story is self-defeating — when that story is causing problems and undermining our goals and happiness — we learn to "drop it" and tell a different, more-productive, more-effective story.

All events are processed and interpreted through the lens of our individual identities, our complex emotional reactions, and the context of our life in order to fit a particular version of reality, the one we believe to be true. So are we telling ourselves stories of abundance or scarcity, happiness or unhappiness, power or powerlessness? Accountability also resides in the midst of our stories. What story are we holding ourselves and others accountable for? Facts matter. Truth matters. We need precision. At the same time, when it comes to accountability, compassion is an essential ingredient for getting at the facts, the truth, in ways that cultivate understanding, alignment, and more effectively working and living together.

All events are processed and interpreted through the lens of our individual identities.... So are we telling ourselves stories of abundance or scarcity, happiness or unhappiness, power or powerlessness?

The Buddha had a good deal to say about how our mind works and how our interpretation of events impacts our experience. In particular, the Buddha focused on how we create pain and suffering for ourselves. He wrote:

> All experience is preceded by mind,
> Led by mind,
> Made by mind.
> Speak or act with a corrupted mind,
> And suffering follows
> As the wagon wheel follows the hoof of an ox.
> All experience is preceded by mind,
> Led by mind,
> Made by mind.
> Speak or act with a peaceful mind,
> And happiness follows.
> Like a never-departing shadow.

The Buddha's core teaching was about finding clarity through self-awareness as a path for reducing suffering. This involves paying attention to the language we use when we speak to ourselves, which has a tremendous influence on how we relate to others and how we move through our daily lives. This includes acknowledging our particular history and place in society, our cultural perspective, our relative strengths and weaknesses, and what we consider meaningful and sacred. This also entails identifying any mistaken beliefs we hold about ourselves, such as the need to achieve some specific goal or standard in order to be seen as competent, to belong, or to be accepted and loved. Everyone develops limiting or mistaken beliefs. This is built into the process of how we make meaning. A core competency of "drop the story" is to question our beliefs, to loosen our attachment to our own stories, to not be overly convinced that our version of ourselves, others, and the world is 100 percent accurate and true all the time.

My father had the mistaken belief that he was a failure. This identity was based on some yardstick he held up as the true measure of success in the world; this involved some combination of money, power, and accomplishment that, in all likelihood, he would never have been able to satisfy. Further, not only did he label himself as a loser, but he labeled our whole family that way. And even when our family had just won ten thousand dollars, that event only reinforced his belief in our failure. There are events, and the interpretation of those events.

Homer Simpson got it half right when he said: "Facts are meaningless. You could use facts to prove anything that's even remotely true!"

In the end, facts aren't meaningless, but their meaning is open to interpretation. We use them to tell the story we prefer.

The Ladder of Inference: Why Our Stories Seem True

The core skill of "drop the story" is to develop awareness of our story-making impulse and of the stories we tell and to learn how to let stories go or revise them when they don't serve us. By that I mean any story that limits us, that narrowly defines our capabilities, that makes change or success seem impossible, or that gets in the way of fostering more effective and trusting relationships.

As Buddha and Alice remind us, the world is not what it seems. Each of us sees and interprets the world through our own personal lens. But through attention, understanding, and practice, we can change the lens, like putting on different glasses, and adjust our particular interpretation of reality. The less-than-good news is that changing how we see ourselves and the world takes effort, practice, and community. This practice can be slippery and seemingly impossible at times — like trying to see our own eyes — which, of course, we never will. We can only see the reflection of our eyes. So how do we get outside our subjective view in order to experience our own experience? This chapter presents several methods — in particular, meditation and mindfulness — but another is learning how the mind filters experience in order to make meaning and formulate beliefs in the first place.

Psychologist and leading organizational development pioneer Chris Argyris developed an excellent model for this he calls the ladder of inference. This model illustrates how we winnow all the "facts" and "events" we experience, choose which ones to pay attention to, decide what those facts mean, and from this develop beliefs about who we are and how the world works in order to make choices about what to do. This mental process begins in the unconscious, or outside of conscious awareness. We automatically sift facts before we even realize we are doing it. Further, these unconscious choices of what to pay attention to tend to reflect our previous experience, or what in the past we have already decided is meaningful and significant. In this way, almost inevitably, this process tends to reinforce the beliefs we already have — by preselecting the facts that support them — until eventually our beliefs come to seem like facts themselves. Our subjective view appears like objective reality, as if our beliefs are no longer "beliefs" but true statements about ourselves and the world. This process continues unless we consciously interrupt it or "drop the story."

See the figure "The Ladder of Inference" below, which shows the various stages of this process.

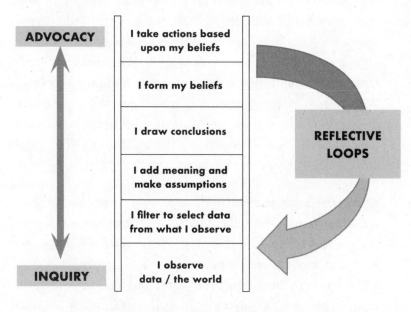

Figure 3. The Ladder of Inference

Observing data: The bottom rung of the ladder is as though there were a video camera recording all the available data. It's like a fire hose of perception, without any narrowing or discernment. This includes everything that our senses take in.

Selecting data: The second rung of the ladder is the process of selecting important data from all the data that is available. We usually don't consciously think about or experience this process. It happens automatically or nearly automatically from the day we are born. For instance, when we walk into a room with many people, we block out most of the people except for the person we are there to meet. Or, as I'm writing now, I'm in my living room, looking at my computer and not taking in the myriad amount of sensory information from my home or the world outside my windows. This process demonstrates the way that we play an active role in creating our worlds. We learn to pay attention to some things and not others as a matter of course. We automatically select data that pertains to keeping safe and staying alive. And we automatically ignore whatever doesn't seem important, isn't a threat, doesn't give pleasure, or isn't something we need.

Adding meaning and making assumptions: Once we have selected particular data, the next rung of the ladder refers to the process of creating meaning. We humans are profound meaning makers and storytellers, yet initially, this also often happens outside of our conscious choice or awareness. In essence, we pay attention to certain data because previous experience has already ascribed it with meaning. This usually relates to what we want or don't want. For instance, meeting a person in a crowded room, we are filled with thoughts and impressions about how we are being received and how we are showing up to meet this person.

In other words, our brains are constantly making predictions about cause and effect, or what will happen next based on the facts. This is incredibly useful and effective.

When walking, we predict where our next step will land. Depending on which handle on the faucet we turn, we predict whether hot or cold water will come out. In our relationships, we predict what people will say or do based on what we've seen them say or do in the past, or based on what we've seen other people say or do.

Drawing conclusions: Having selected certain data as important and meaningful, based on established assumptions, we draw certain conclusions depending on whether our assumptions are correct. In a more conscious or aware way, our narrative begins to take shape, the story that supports our beliefs. If our assumptions are correct, and they are most of the time, that reinforces what we know. If not, and this causes real problems, we have to figure out what went wrong. Did we misunderstand the data or overlook something we didn't realize was important? Do we need to change our assumptions or beliefs to make room for this new information, or did someone else do something wrong, and they need to be corrected? In relationships, false assumptions are fertile ground for the development of misalignments and conflicts.

Forming beliefs: The next rung is forming beliefs. Our stories become further solidified regarding how we believe we, others, and the world function. Based on a largely unconscious process of observation and prediction, we form beliefs about how individuals, groups, organizations, and societies will behave.

Taking action: With our beliefs firmly established, we now can make plans, take action, and respond the best way we know how in order to live a happy and successful life. That is the function of this whole cognitive process: It helps guide our actions so we succeed. The trouble is, even when our beliefs are no longer helping us to take effective action to solve problems, we rarely question them. This is usually because we have stopped recognizing our beliefs as something we've created and thus something we can change. We become stuck in a closed loop.

A Closed Loop

A core aspect of the ladder of inference model is that the process can become a closed loop. That is, once we form our beliefs, we rarely revisit the bottom rung of the ladder. We don't try to observe the widest data set of information. Instead, by automatically selecting only a narrow slice of information to pay attention to, we narrow our understandings and our world.

Dropping the story means being curious about the basis of our beliefs. It means noticing the fact that we are always selecting data, adding meaning, making assumptions, translating what's learned into beliefs, and using those beliefs to guide our actions. Dropping the story is a way to short-circuit this largely automatic process so that we observe ourselves, others, and the world as if for the first time, accessing the widest possible data set. It means simply noticing what we are thinking and feeling, whatever that might be, whether it's happiness or sadness, joy or pain or grief. This practice of noticing without judgment, without pushing certain feelings away or overly identifying with others, is a core practice of finding clarity.

Identity: The Story of Ourselves

Our stories shape our underlying identities and our underlying identities shape our stories. Our identities are the stories we tell ourselves about who we are. We create our identities through the lens of what is most important to us, what matters most. As we seek to find more clarity, our challenge is to be an observer of our subjective self. To do this, we need practices that help us be more like a clear pond, practices that enable us to both see ourselves and see through our stories and identity.

The power and leverage of dropping our story is that it keeps us from being entrenched in limited, ineffective stories and beliefs. We learn how to take control of our story so we can change it and tell the stories that we most deeply aspire to tell and embody. Perhaps some of these stories, these limited identities, sound familiar:

- I'm stressed out a lot of the time and want to find more spaciousness.
- I don't have much influence and would like to have more.
- I'm not good at learning new skills and want to be a better learner.
- I'm not a good writer and want to improve.
- I'm not very athletic and want to enjoy working out and sports.
- I'm not very flexible in my thinking and want to see from a wider perspective.

It takes practice to shift our identity, to become more the person we aspire to be. The practice of effectively shifting identity contains these four elements, which the rest of the chapter explores:

> The power and leverage of dropping our story is that it keeps us from being entrenched in limited, ineffective stories and beliefs.

Practicing meditation: Meditation practice offers a profound opportunity to become radically familiar with our stories and to go beyond them. Vastly misunderstood, meditation, though it has many benefits, is a profound practice that provides insight into how we create our identities. Meditation includes resetting and renewing; it's a practice of returning to zero that is often left out of conventional identity shift and professional development strategies.

Identifying limiting stories and mistaken beliefs: Another important effort is to recognize and name limiting stories and mistaken beliefs. As we bring awareness to the messages we sometimes unconsciously tell ourselves, we gain insight into core principles we may have lost sight of. Then we can change those stories and beliefs and open to a wider, clearer view.

Creating a development plan: As we gain more insight into ourselves and our mistaken beliefs, we can create a development plan for furthering our awareness and changing our perspective and behavior. We develop a plan for transforming pain into possibilities.

Cultivating self-compassion and letting go of negative stories: Throughout this process, we have the opportunity to practice self-compassion. We can loosen the incessant inner critic or inner judge that beckons us to be protective and narrow and to avoid change. As this voice quiets, we find it easier to let go of what doesn't serve us.

Practicing Meditation

When people tell me that they don't have time to meditate, I think of Yuval Noah Harari's book *21 Lessons for the 21st Century*. His twenty-first lesson is meditation. Harari shares that he meditates for two hours most days, and that he could not have written his two groundbreaking, best-selling (and very dense) books *Sapiens* and *Homo Deus* without his daily meditation practice. Many people treat meditation practice as if it were extra, something that takes time away from their lives, or like another item on their already full to-do lists. Yes, it does take time, but so does putting oil in the car and air in the tires. If we didn't engage in regular automobile maintenance, our cars would stop running and take a lot more of our time.

Meditation practice is highly misunderstood and undervalued for its true purpose: its potent, life-changing benefits. To me, meditation apps and most conventional, guided meditations are like the "gateway drug" for discovering what meditation is actually capable of. However, if meditation is just another activity someone does, no different from an hour completing tasks, then it may result in little real shifting or personal change.

Of course, meditation provides a number of physical and mental health benefits: It can reduce stress, improve memory, increase attention, lessen anxiety, and inspire better sleep. These benefits are all good, useful, and important.

But to truly find clarity and develop compassionate accountability, I encourage you to explore a different relationship
with meditation.

The Real Reason to Meditate

The real impact and benefit, the surprising magic, of meditation practice is that it enables you to go deeper — to
know yourself and to go beyond your usual sense of self.
Meditation is less like going to the gym to build muscles
and more like a process of transformation that goes to the
very root of who you are and how you engage with yourself and your environment. Very few gyms have this kind
of transformation in mind.

Shunryu Suzuki, the founder of the San Francisco Zen
Center, explained that to meditate is to let go of all expectations with each exhale. This may sound easy, but it's challenging to let go of our to-do lists, our projects, our self-help
plans, and the various expectations, hopes, and dreams we
have for today, tomorrow, and our future. Our expectations
and future live within us and are powerfully embedded in
every breath we take. Suzuki proposed that meditation is
to work at this level of our being, of our consciousness. He
wrote, "With each exhale, let go of everything, including
the idea that there will be another inhale. Let yourself die
with each exhale. Then, if another inhale arrives, be surprised, and say to yourself, 'Oh, I'm here, I'm still alive.'"

This approach to meditation is a radical renewal of our
"big mind"; it helps create a more full-functioning mind.
This is the transformative power of meditation. It's the
ability to shift from an ordinary way of being to becoming
more present, with greater care and respect for everything

and for yourself. It is a way of hitting the reset button, to start over, refreshed. It is a way of practicing, cultivating, and reinforcing the practice "drop the story."

I strongly suggest starting a regular meditation practice, using whatever method works best for you. Meditation doesn't have to be long; even ten to twenty minutes a day provides benefits. For more on creating a dedicated space for meditation, see "Renewal: Everywhere You Go Is Your Temple," page 149.

Whatever your practice consists of, here are some of the underlying elements and guidelines with this approach to meditation:

No expectations: Though some expectation or motivation brings us to meditation practice, the practice itself is to let go of expecting anything or attempting to change. Expectations are by definition a form of waiting for something to happen: "I'll be happy and satisfied when," or "I'll be successful when." Meditation is cultivating the quality and ability to give up and let go; to loosen and shift your relationship with your thoughts, feelings, and opinions, right now.

Changing your view of self: Meditation supports a radical sense of our own ability to take ownership of our thoughts and feelings. This experience can shift how we see ourselves, others, and the world.

Increasing sincerity: A regular meditation practice can bolster an experience of caring, of sincerity, of wholeheartedness and warmheartedness, as a way of living our daily lives.

Emotional freedom: Meditation helps us tune in to our emotions and have more choice in how to respond. For example, we can learn to notice as anger (or any emotion) arises in our body, and meditation helps us pause without overreacting or underreacting, so we can decide what to say and do to achieve the best possible outcome for all involved.

Nondual approach: Meditation practice is a way of cultivating a radically different approach to our usual judgments of good and bad, right and wrong, as well as birth and death. We train ourselves to see ourselves and the world through the lens of acceptance and profound curiosity, training our minds and bodies to appreciate everything: distractions, pain, joy, grief, and being alive, right now.

The Heart Sutra: A Story for Dropping Our Story

A practice that supports integrating insights from meditation into your work and life is to study and vocalize inspiring words or sacred texts. One such text is the Heart Sutra, which is a very powerful, short, almost poem-like piece that supports this practice of dropping the story. Repeating any part of this text regularly, as one part of an ongoing meditation practice, can help transform the language you use when thinking about yourself and the story you tell about who you are.

In the Zen tradition, practice centers read or chant this short, two-thousand-year-old text every day, sometimes several times a day. While the term *sutra* refers to a teaching from the historical Buddha, this particular text was clearly written hundreds of years after the time of Buddha's life, most likely in India during the first or second century. The word *heart* implies that this is an expression of the heart of the Buddha's teachings.

The Heart Sutra is both radical and practical. It's an actionable teaching on the practice of dropping the story. One line goes like this: "No form, no sensation, no perception, no formation, no consciousness; no eyes, no ears, no nose, no tongue, no body, no mind; no sight, no sound, no smell, no taste, no touch, no object of mind."

This list names various concepts and processes that contribute to our sense of self. Negating them implies that even what we think of as us, our sense of self, our usual experience of a solid, unchanging identity, is a story. By breaking the "story" of self into separate components, we get some insight into the process of how we each create this story of I, me, the self. This useful, important insight helps loosen even our most basic sense of self; we practice seeing our perceptions as interpretations, which creates some space between our perception and our story. This sutra evokes an existential question: What if everything that we think of as real and solid, all the stories we tell ourselves about what we see, hear, feel, taste, and touch, don't exist in the way we take for granted, in the way we assume is obvious and real? What if all our perceptions are interpretations of reality? What if the world is not as it seems?

Elsewhere, the Heart Sutra has this line: "There is neither ignorance nor extinction of ignorance ... neither what we think of as old age and death nor extinction of what we think of as old age and death."

In typical Zen fashion, the Heart Sutra evokes a paradox. This line reverses the previous negations and asks: Well, what if everything is exactly as we think and perceive?

What if the world is as it seems? That is, don't get too carried away or too attached to any story, including the story that our perceptions are always wrong. Sometimes, what we perceive and think and feel might be correct and sometimes it might not be. Don't be caught by assumptions. Stay open. Go deeper. Train the mind to not be limited by stories.

In the middle of the Heart Sutra is another important line: "Without hindrance, there is no fear." This summarizes this practice of "drop the story." The point is to become more clear, open, flexible, full-functioning, and compassionate, by noticing and letting go of the stories, beliefs, and fears that hinder us. I've included my own rendition of the Heart Sutra in appendix 1. Spend some time with it. Read it and memorize a line or two that speak to you. Attempt to understand it and let go of trying to understand it. See how you are influenced by the Heart Sutra and the practice of "the world is not what it seems."

Identifying Mistaken Beliefs

What stories do you tell yourself when you see yourself, others, and the world? Of course, our stories aren't one-dimensional or static, but many-layered and contextual. We tell different stories depending on the myriad circumstances we encounter. And we each develop our own patterns, strengths, blind spots, and growth areas. Most often, do you see through the lens of curiosity or anger, of scarcity or abundance, of anxiety or ease? Do you assume the best or worst of others? As a leader, do you lead by controlling what others do or by fostering group connections and individual agency?

Mistaken beliefs are limiting beliefs based on particular

needs and patterns of avoidance. We adopt these mistaken beliefs thinking they will support us to be safer, to enhance our feeling of belonging, and to be more loved. Instead, they narrow our vision of ourselves and negatively impact our ability to communicate with more freedom and with compassionate accountability.

Here are some common mistaken beliefs (originally inspired by the Enneagram):

- We are not accepted for who we are.
- We have to be needed in order to be loved.
- We are valued for what we do, not who we are.
- We are missing something important and are misunderstood.
- We need to accumulate knowledge to be loved and accepted.
- We live in a primarily unfair and untrustworthy world and need to pursue security.
- We live in a frustrating and limiting world.
- We need to create comfort and avoid conflict as a substitute for love.

From our core mistaken beliefs, we each adopt a strategy and direct our energy toward certain behaviors and communication styles, and we each develop certain avoidance patterns. These patterns, of what we are drawn to and what we avoid, are not character flaws, but they are survival patterns that nearly everyone adopts. Once we recognize patterns, we can work with them more skillfully and improve how we communicate.

To use a personal example, I've learned that a mistaken belief that I work with is around my need for comfort. I have a strong tendency to ignore stress and anxiety and avoid conflict, thinking that this is what I need to do to be loved and for everything to work out well. Recognizing this mistaken belief has made an enormous difference for me as a leader. I'm now better able to loosen the stories I tell myself in the moment, which allows me to let go of my attachment to comfort so I can meet conflict in the moment and have more genuine and effective conversations with my colleagues. My leadership and my relationships with my coworkers have greatly improved as I have found clarity about this mistaken belief and other proclivities and patterns.

Finding clarity about our own mistaken beliefs and loosening our stories can also help us recognize the patterns and proclivities of the people we work and live with. For example, my wife has many of the opposite tendencies from mine. One of her mistaken beliefs is that the world tends to be unjust and that her job is to protect others. She tends to embrace conflict, and she can be rather intense and intimidating at times. We have both learned and grown immensely from seeing how our different patterns play out in our relationship.

The point of delving into these mistaken beliefs and behavioral tendencies is to increase our understanding by developing more insight into the patterns that influence our needs, our fears, and ultimately our identity. Through greater understanding, we can then plan for how to work and live with others with more clarity, effectiveness, and joy.

Creating a Behavioral Development Plan

You may already know what some of your mistaken beliefs are. However, to help identify them and, more importantly, to shift and change these proclivities, I encourage you to create a behavioral development plan. This may sound official or formal, but it's really just a way to make your intentions concrete by setting goals for yourself.

To start, reflect upon your strengths. If you wish, write these down. Acknowledge what people appreciate about you and your communication style. Notice what's working well, both in how you feel about yourself and in your most important relationships. In essence, the goal of your plan is to build upon these strengths and add new ones.

At the same time, be curious about your story and any negative tendencies and proclivities that limit you, narrow your vision, and hold you back. If you wish, write these down as well. Generally, there is no lack of signs or signals around limiting beliefs. We recognize them when we pay attention to the feedback we receive from our own feelings and by assessing the quality of our relationships at work, at home, and in all parts of our lives. Identifying hindrances, limiting stories, and mistaken beliefs is useful and important information. It shows us exactly what we want to change.

Next, create a behavioral development plan that lists the actions and activities that you want to pursue to cultivate greater awareness, curiosity, and freedom. There is no particular format you need to follow. This is entirely personal and embodies whatever might work best for you. However, I encourage you to be specific and detailed: Write what you will do, for how long, and when, either by the day, week, or month.

Here are some elements or categories I suggest considering, along with examples of what they might consist of.

In each of these activities, explore your stretch zone, experimenting with more depth or intensity.

Meditation: This might be the most important practice for finding clarity and dropping the story. Ideally, several days a week (or every day) include a short meditation practice. I like to start my day with a twenty- to thirty-minute meditation, but do whatever works and is sustainable for you. Find a way to do retreats: half-day, one-day, or multiday silent retreats.

Study: Read almost every day, even if it is only for a few minutes. Choose books from spirituality, leadership, or literature that expand your world. Create a reading list, and then develop a regular reading practice.

Work: Bring an approach of compassionate accountability into your day-to-day work. Contextualize your work as a place to learn, grow, and develop yourself as well as to support others. Aspire to be happy and fulfilled at work, and notice and learn from the gaps between what is and your aspirations.

Conflict: Bring awareness to conflicts and challenging relationships and situations. Notice any tendencies to avoid conflict or to seek it. Consider whether there are other ways to effectively engage with conflict that are outside of your comfort zone; explore these.

Relationships: Listen more deeply to yourself and others. Be more curious about your experience of the people you work with and of family members and friends. See each conversation as a learning opportunity.

Sleep: Make sleep a critical part of your development plan. Be curious about the amount and quality of your sleep. Be curious about your dreams and about your state of mind when waking up.

Pleasure: Do enjoyable activities every day. Our emotional fortitude and flexibility improve when we are open, curious, and happy. What brings you joy? More often than not, do those things.

Self-Compassion: Letting Go of Negative Stories

One of the most powerful and pervasive stories we humans tend to have is the story of the inner critic. This is the inner judge, the voice of criticism scanning for threats — *Do I look all right? What if I fail? What might go wrong?* This voice can get downright mean: *You are so dumb — how could you do that!?*

One of the greatest underlying causes of bad behavior, conflicts, and misunderstandings comes from not accepting ourselves and not liking ourselves. A common mistaken belief is that we need to be self-critical, which can lead to various forms of self-loathing. The Dalai Lama was once answering questions from a large American audience. Someone asked him what to do about self-loathing. He was puzzled, very puzzled, not fully understanding what the person meant. Apparently, there is no similar word for self-loathing in the Tibetan language. The Dalai Lama was surprised how common this emotion is in the United States.

Self-compassion is the antidote to the many forms of not accepting ourselves. It is a simple and powerful way to address and shift our inner conflicts and self-criticisms. With self-compassion, we work on ourselves using the most leverage by focusing on the place where the smallest changes can have the most impact — practicing compassionate accountability with ourselves.

Self-Compassion Meditation

Here is another form of guided meditation, one that cultivates the practice of self-compassion. Our inner critic or inner judge is fundamentally a way to keep us safe and protect us from getting hurt. But it has a way of narrowing our vision and clogging up our efforts to widen our story about ourselves and our relationships.

This meditation practice is meant to last about fifteen minutes and proceed through three stages. Each involves focusing on the breath in a certain way for about five minutes. Either lying down or in a comfortable seated position, with eyes closed or open, do this for the first five minutes:

- With each inhale, bring awareness to the fact that you are breathing.
- With each exhale, let go of everything and empty out, breathe out fully.

For the following five minutes, become self-reflective of how you feel in this moment:

- Bring curiosity to each inhale and exhale — what is your experience? What is it like to be here, alive, without trying to change anything?
- Begin to cultivate a quality of kindness, self-acceptance, and love for yourself. Experiment with putting one of your hands on your chest.

During the last five minutes or so, do the following:

- With each inhale, explore feeling safe and satisfied, accept yourself and love yourself. Notice what this feels like.
- With each exhale, let go of everything and empty out, breathe out fully.

The Story I'm Telling Myself Is...

Regularly practicing the self-compassion meditation or repeating the Heart Sutra are paths and practices for finding more clarity and greater freedom, for dropping or at least loosening our story. Treating our stories as real or fixed limits us, especially those stories that get in the way of becoming the person we aspire to be. Loosening our tight hold on our identity allows us to explore and play more with how we see ourselves.

However, another useful practice is to articulate the negative story or mistaken belief that our emotions or actions embody. Then, once we name that story, we can express a different, positive story, the one we want to live by.

This shift in language is more than semantics or positive thinking. It teaches us to recognize what is and to name how we want to change. Experiment with this practice and see whether it's useful.

First, when you notice a mistaken belief or negative story, articulate it using the phrase, "The story I'm telling myself is..." For example:

If you write, but don't think of yourself as a writer, you can say to yourself: The story I'm telling myself is that I'm not a writer.

>If you influence those you work with, but don't see yourself as a leader, you can say to yourself: The story I'm telling myself is that I'm not a leader.
>
>If you run, but don't see yourself as a runner, you can say to yourself: The story I'm telling myself is that I'm not an athlete.
>
>If you feel too busy and like you never have enough of what you need, you can say to yourself: The story I'm telling myself is that I lack time and spaciousness.

Initially, once you identify a mistaken belief, simply recognize it as such; use this practice to explore your existing sense of self or identity.

This practice can also be extremely valuable when working with conflicts or disagreements with other people. If you are feeling hurt and angry about something someone else has said or done, identify the cause and then use the same prompt: The story I'm telling myself is ...

>My feelings were hurt when you didn't invite me to your event. The story I'm telling myself is that I'm not important to you.
>
>I felt angry during our meeting this morning when my ideas were dismissed. The story I'm telling myself is that my contributions aren't valued by our team.

This small shift in language has enormous leverage. It can help us create a sense of safety, take responsibility for our perceptions, and lay the foundation for greater understanding and alignment. By voicing that this reaction is a story means that you are not insisting that your version of events is necessarily accurate and true, that you are right (and someone else is wrong). Of course, it takes courage to open in this way, but this openness can help us embrace a different, more-positive, more-effective story.

The Story I Want to Live By Is ...

The practice of dropping the story doesn't mean we drop all stories or have no story. As I say, humans are storytellers. We need stories. But we need stories that help us see more clearly and act more effectively to achieve our aspirations and goals. Once you have identified "the story I am telling myself," replace it by finishing the prompt: "The story I want to live by is ..."

Here are some suggestions for the kinds of positive stories you might want to live by:

- Every moment is new, rich, and surprising.
- My life and all lives are sacred.
- Work is a terrific cauldron for personal, professional, and spiritual development.
- I can learn and grow from pain, disappointment, and grief.
- I am confident and humble at the same time.
- I love playing and being active and I love being still and quiet.

I understand that the practice of dropping the story is at times challenging or daunting. So approach this practice with curiosity, like Alice, in this exchange with the doorknob:

ALICE: I simply must get through!

DOORKNOB: Sorry, you're much too big. Simply impassable!

ALICE: You mean impossible.

DOOR: No, impassable. Nothing's impossible!

3

Listen for Understanding

Tangles everywhere.
People are entangled in a tangle.
I ask you this: Who can untangle the tangles?

The Buddha responds:
A person established in integrity,
developing clarity of mind;
a person who recognizes and transforms greed, hatred,
   and confusion:
for them, the tangle is untangled.

— from the Jata Sutta, an ancient Pali text

When I lead two-day mindful leadership trainings, I usually give some suggested homework, generally in the form of practices, at the conclusion of the first day. Often I say, "When you go home this evening, if your partner or a close friend says they want to speak with you about a challenge or problem, instead of launching into problem-solving mode, try this. Ask them, 'Would you like me to just listen, or would you like me to problem solve with you?'"

The next morning, I begin the second day of training by asking how the homework went. Typically, several participants — more often men, sometimes a woman — say that their partners were quite pleased and immensely surprised. "My wife didn't recognize me!" a middle-aged computer engineer once reported. "She asked if I'd been taken over by some aliens during the workshop."

We all laughed at our collective human tendency to not listen and instead launch right into solving other people's problems. Listening sounds so simple and straightforward, so easy. It is. Most of the time ...

What is it that makes listening so powerful? Is it just the fact of silence, of not talking? Homer Simpson apparently believes this, having once said, "Just because I don't care doesn't mean I'm not listening."

As usual, Homer identifies the right issue but learns the wrong lesson: The quality of our listening inevitably demonstrates the quality of our caring. That's what this chapter explores — how to use the quality of our listening to care with curiosity about other's stories, our stories, and what we might be missing.

> As usual, Homer identifies the right issue but learns the wrong lesson: The quality of our listening inevitably demonstrates the quality of our caring.

Untangle the Tangles

One thing we learn very quickly when we ask people to share their experiences, and then listen openly to their replies, is that everyone has their own perspective, their own understanding of the world and its problems. Indeed, it can be shocking how differently people can view the same situation, the same reality we all share.

Alice captures this quite well. As she says: "If I had a world of my own, everything would be nonsense. Nothing would be what it is because everything would be what it isn't. And contrariwise, what it is, it wouldn't be. And what it wouldn't be, it would. You see?"

I have had conversations with others that went something like Alice's. The reality I thought I understood was turned upside down or inside out by someone else's point of view. As we talk, I realize our understandings have gotten tangled not unlike a computer cord in a backpack. When we put it away, it seemed fine, but when we retrieve it, the cord has mysteriously become tangled with knots that would stymie a Boy Scout. In the world of farming, there is even an expression for this — "gone haywire." When you cut the metal wires holding bales of hay together and don't carefully put them away, chaos ensues.

Even with great care and the best of intentions, relationships can become quite tangled, out of alignment, and fraught with conflict. At times, this happens when people behave badly — when they distort the truth, lie, deceive, abuse power, break agreements, and undercut trust. Relationship tangles can result from broken commitments, conflicting agendas, pent-up anger or frustration, and other forms of feeling let down or of letting others down. Tangles are often caused by some form of misunderstanding or a lack of understanding. Most directly, they arise from a lack of listening, which is like putting away a cord in a backpack without securing it from unraveling.

Tangles happen strangely often and unexpectedly in our most important relationships, whether at work, with friends, or within families. Many tangles occur unintentionally from people having different experiences. The same words, the same actions, can be seen, felt, and understood in completely different ways. This can be confusing, frustrating, and even infuriating. Rather than react with curiosity, rather than ask someone why they feel the way they do, we can become angry, defensive, and argumentative. We might insist on our point of view while denying or discrediting the other person's. These disagreements can sometimes be relatively minor and easy to overcome, but at times, they can result in profound and irreparable breaks.

We might share the insight of psychiatrist R. D. Laing, describing the uniqueness of how we each perceive the world:

> I cannot experience your experience.
> You cannot experience my experience.
> Therefore, we are invisible to each other.

Tangles and misunderstanding are particularly prevalent in our workplaces, where the stakes are high, the pace is accelerated, and people are working together within hierarchies of power and responsibility. This combination provides a particularly rich cauldron for challenging relationships. The primary reason people feel stressed and unhappy, or leave their jobs, is from feeling disconnected or in conflict with those they work for and with. Tangles everywhere.

That said, most workplaces aspire to align around goals and objectives; they seek consensus and agreement with a multitude of decisions. People often work within teams, work across a variety of functions and skill sets, and sometimes work globally across cultures. Additionally, people bring their own sense of identity, their own particular communication styles, and their own emotional awareness and development. Our lives are filled with desires, fears, traumas, and visions of what's possible.

Anxiety Makes It Hard to Hear Others

There is no shortage of stress and anxiety in the workplace. Working virtually from home and working in different time zones and across a variety of functions can accentuate this stress and anxiety. Working and leading with anxiety can become habitual, invisible, and an accepted norm. However, anxiety can make us defensive. I once had a senior banking executive in one of my mindful leadership workshops share that he spent nearly 90 percent of his time "protecting his back" from political conflicts within his organization. Similarly, we can feel like we always have to be protecting ourselves, either from attack or failure. Anxiety breeds mistrust and doubt, which makes it hard to hear what others are saying. And this failure to listen often creates the very tangles we're anxious to avoid.

For example, Frank had worked at a major airport for fifteen years and had recently been promoted to lead an operations team. I was brought in by the human resources department after several members of Frank's team reported that they didn't trust Frank and at times didn't feel safe at work.

I interviewed Frank's team members, who said they felt that Frank was not a good listener. They also described situations in which he had emotional outbursts of anger and frustration. "He seems tense, nearly all the time," one of his direct reports told me. "He also seems distracted, as though his attention is not with me and what I'm saying."

When I spoke with Frank, I found that, as with many leaders and managers, he was leading with anxiety. His inner dialogue focused primarily on how he was doing, and he was continually worried about making mistakes and failing. He spent most of his time reliving and ruminating about the past (and what he wished he had done differently) and worrying about the future (by imagining what could go wrong).

Of course, working in an airport can be stressful. Airplanes are landing literally every few minutes. There is a constant awareness that one's job includes matters of life and death. So it's essential that everyone learn from the past, anticipate what might go wrong in the future, and take whatever corrective adjustments and actions are necessary to ensure that everything goes smoothly and safely. That applies not just to airports, but to the business world in general. In almost every workplace, anxiety comes with the territory, which makes it all the more important not to let anxiety dominate our thoughts and interactions, since it can undermine our ability to see clearly and foster effective teamwork.

Frank was really surprised to hear that others perceived him as not being a good listener. He disagreed strongly and presented his case for why he thought others were wrong. Eventually, I told him, "Frank, if you think you are a good listener, and the people around you say you are not a good listener, then you are not a good listener." This certainly got his attention, and as we talked further, he committed to changing his behavior. He agreed that his anxiety, while understandable, was undermining his ability to genuinely listen to his team and foster a safe, trusting environment.

Cultivating trust and a sense of safety is another way to characterize what compassionate accountability means. One important way we create this is through the quality of our listening. If, like Homer, we "listen" without caring, that fosters mistrust and cynicism. Others recognize that what they say has little or no impact and that their opinions, perspective, and knowledge are not valued. This encourages a "me-first" attitude in which everyone looks out mainly for themselves, since they can't trust the group to protect them or care about them. Self-interest is real and an important aspect of business, but so is common interest, or the shared goals and values that inspire us to work together as a team (or a family). When we listen openly, with curiosity, we widen our perspective, enabling our ability to identify what's best for the group, what's best for the relationships between individuals, and what's best for each person. We also can encourage others to listen openly, with curiosity, creating a virtuous circle of compassionate accountability.

Types of Listening

Who is this miracle speaking to me?
And who is this miracle listening?
What amazingness are we creating?
Out of gray matter a star spark of thought

leaps between synapses into the air,
and pours through gray matter, into my heart:
how can I not listen generously?

— Marilyn Nelson

Listening may be the strongest antidote for preventing tangled relationships and for untangling tangles once they occur. Then again, not all listening is the same. If we want to find clarity with others and cultivate compassionate accountability, we need to listen with genuine caring and curiosity about what others think and feel. This involves dropping our story and being open to the experience of others. It is hard to listen effectively when we hold tightly to our own identity, to our own needs, out of insecurity, anxiety, or fear.

There are various types of listening, and essentially, each type is distinguished by what we are listening for. This can vary depending on the context and the relationship, and except for the first two, the types aren't necessarily better or worse, just different. However, it's helpful to become more curious and more self-aware of the quality of your listening. When someone speaks, are you listening with full openness to whatever they have to say, or are you filled with expectations and are listening for a certain type of information? Further, what message are you trying to convey with the quality of your listening?

Not Listening

This is the form of listening Homer describes, and judging by its prevalence, it's very popular. This is the kind of listening that occurs in countless business meetings when participants check emails, surf the internet, and doodle while others talk. Being physically present, simply hearing someone's words, or waiting for someone to finish talking in order to speak — this does not count as genuine listening.

Listening with Preconceived Ideas

This is a variation of not listening, but with an important distinction. Instead of being distracted or not caring what someone says, this is listening with a fixed mindset. We assume we know what the other person will say, or we have already made up our mind about them and the topic, and as a result, we are not really listening.

Listening for Content

This is a vital form of listening, but it is also limited. This refers to paying attention to the narrative, the story, or the content of what is being said. Of course, this is important. At the same time, if we listen just for content, we may miss the real story.

"I'd like to have the report by Monday morning" is a simple, direct request. A deadline is being communicated. However, many times, maybe even most of the time, people communicate more than the explicit content of the words they speak. A simple directive might contain one or more unspoken messages, and these are usually more important. In this case, if we have been late with previous reports, the underlying message might be: *I am frustrated with your lateness and challenge you to meet this one.* Or if we generally meet deadlines and exceed expectations, the underlying message might be: *I have confidence and trust you'll meet this deadline, even if it's short notice.*

All the forms of listening that follow focus on these often unspoken, underlying messages, which relate to a mixture of feelings, intentions, and identity issues, in addition to listening for alignment and in order to understand the other person's point of view.

Listening for Feelings

We tend to "hear feelings" automatically. We are wired for empathy, to feel the feelings of others. In trainings, when I instruct participants to listen for feelings, I often point out the surprise, the miracle really, that no instructions are required for how to listen for feelings. We all know intuitively how to read nonverbal communication and tone of voice. However, we do need to make some effort to bring our awareness and focus into the realm of feelings. Sometimes, it can be difficult to listen for the feelings of others when our own feelings are particularly strong, or when the content of what someone says is particularly urgent, overwhelming, or compelling.

Listening for Alignment

Part of what it means to listen with curiosity is to listen for where we and others are aligned. When someone describes their vision of success, and how to achieve it, does that match our own? This includes noticing motivations and intentions. Particularly at work, but in any conversation related to goals, taking action, and working together, bring awareness to what you each have in common and also to where there might be gaps in alignment. Notice both, without immediately focusing solely on gaps. For instance, in the above example, notice whether you agree with your supervisor that the report needs to be completed by Monday morning. Notice whether you share the same assessment about what's urgent and needs to be done. Then notice places where there might be a lack of alignment. For instance, you might agree that the report is needed by Monday, but disagree that you alone can accomplish that (whether your supervisor has confidence in you or not). Perhaps you can't complete your work without more data from others, or perhaps you have other commitments that conflict with your ability to meet this timetable. By sharing your assessment of where you and your supervisor are and are not aligned, that will help you both focus on resolving problems — whether by renegotiating timeframes, getting more help, or revising goals.

Sometimes, gaps in alignment can be large and surprising. We can think: *Wow. Isn't that interesting and amazing that this person has such a different experience and expectation!* Ideally, fostering the mindset of curiosity when listening for alignment helps us minimize reactivity and see gaps more clearly.

Listening for Intentions

Listening for intentions is about focusing on what is most important to the other person, whether they are expressing that openly or not. We pay attention to the underlying "why." Why is this person telling us certain information, for what purpose? Why is their version of events important to them? What values are they expressing? Of course, this can also include listening for alignment: Do we share the same opinion about what's important? Do we have similar core values?

Listening for Identity Issues

Issues of identity are often the most powerful drivers of conflict. In the world of work, the most common identity issue concerns competence. That is, we are very sensitive to whether others regard us as competent or not, and an unspoken, underlying question is often: *Am I doing my job well? Am I succeeding or failing? Did I make a mistake or not understand?* These can quickly turn into a matter of identity: *Am I competent? Am I a success or a failure?*

In families and important relationships, competence may be one of a host of complex issues, but the core identity issue often boils down to: *Am I loved and am I lovable?*

Listening for Understanding

When we listen for understanding, we drop into our heart center. We seek to feel the feelings of the other person, putting ourselves in their shoes as much as possible. The intention isn't only to understand, but also to foster a genuine connection, to help and to heal. Listening for understanding is an expression of compassion as well as accountability. We desire to feel, understand, clarify, and help — all at the same time.

> Listening for understanding is an expression of compassion as well as accountability. We desire to feel, understand, clarify, and help — all at the same time.

In a way, listening for understanding incorporates all the various positive types of listening. We are the most openly curious, which helps create an environment in which people feel safe enough to be vulnerable and share honestly. This in itself is an expression of caring. Making sure someone hears that message can be as important as — or even more important than — whatever is said. All genuine listening seeks greater clarity, but when listening embodies caring, we foster the ability to untangle the tangles together.

Focus First on Relationships, Not Roles

A practice that improves the quality of our listening is to focus on valuing relationships, not fulfilling particular roles. This is a form of dropping our story. When listening, we put aside preconceived ideas and expectations based on roles — such as boss/employee, parent/child, and so on. Instead, our intention is simply to see, feel, and listen with an open mind and heart to the person in front of us, not knowing for the moment what will happen or what we will do with whatever is shared. This means setting aside any urge to defend ourselves and letting go of being right, and instead listening, really listening, with care and compassion.

This doesn't mean we ignore discernment or pretend that roles don't exist. Rather, we acknowledge different roles, accept them, and put them aside in order to listen without judgment and to foster a sense of caring and safety.

In the workplace, it is easy to lose sight that we are working with fellow human beings. We can start to regard people as little more than their titles — the CEO, the customer service manager, the executive assistant. These roles define someone's job and workplace responsibilities, how they support the organization, but that is not who they are. It can take some effort to hold these roles more loosely; to lead, work, and live more in relationship. It's much like "taking the board off your shoulder." We see that, no matter what someone's formal or official role, they are a person worthy of relationship.

Bringing awareness to relationships, but without disregarding roles, is another way of embodying compassionate accountability. We listen with compassion, noticing how others are feeling, and with a motivation to help, while also acknowledging accountability, knowing that if actions need to be taken, those actions may be defined by everyone's role.

Acting relationally is a mindset and attitude that is rich and sufficient within itself. It is to be always ready for anything, open to everything. It is the mind of compassion, original and boundless.

Clarity Circles: Personal Sharing to Mine Group Wisdom

For about fifteen years, I've been meeting with a group of peers once a month for three hours. Our goal is simply to help one another meet the varied challenges of life, and I have found this extremely valuable for solving personal problems and supporting my personal, family, and work aspirations. There is something special, unique, and powerful about the wisdom of groups, especially when there is an abundance of care, trust, and listening. The relationships I've built with each person are invaluable.

Some of our meetings are designed as extended check-in

sessions where each person gets a few minutes, or longer, to report on key aspects of their lives — personal, work, and family — and express what's going well, what's not going well, what they are looking forward to, and what they are not looking forward to.

Other times we also engage in the Quaker-based, deep-listening methodology called "clarity circles." To start, one member presents an issue to the group where they need more clarity. They describe this issue uninterrupted, including what questions they have and what help they want. The other members just listen and are then given turns to ask clarifying questions and to share related experiences from their own lives. Two key components of a clarity circle are listening with the spirit of curiosity and refraining from giving direct advice. The emphasis is that each person speaks from their own experience without telling the person what to do. Of course, at times, the person presenting their issue may ask for advice, and this is done with great care.

Appendix 3, "Finding Clarity Group Circles," describes in detail this method of group sharing and listening. However, you can modify this approach in whatever way works for you. In any problem-solving group, whenever anyone asks for your help, practice the same principles of curious listening and personal sharing, rather than advice-giving, and see how it works.

Why Listen? To Build Commitment

In any relationship or group, one fundamental reason to listen for understanding is to cultivate a shared commitment to that relationship or group. That is a critical way to avoid the tangles — particularly misunderstandings, cynicism, and mistrust — in the first place. Building commitment, however, is an ongoing, intertwined process that is based on mutual trust, safety, clarity, compassion, and account-ability, which are all things that listening for understand-ing fosters. Commitment is essential to self-development, to open and healthy relationships, and to creating caring, effective cultures that feel good and do good.

Commitment starts with ourselves. Before we can ask others for their commitment, we must commit ourselves to self-awareness and self-discovery, as well as to understand-ing and seeing the best in others. We commit to working toward alignment and trust, even when there are gaps and conflicts. We commit to the health and well-being of our-selves, our relationships, and the teams and organizations we're part of.

As with listening, commitment comes in a variety of flavors, some of which are really negative forms.

For instance, intending harm is a form of commitment. In my experience, this arises most often as a symptom of feeling unheard and unrecognized, and so someone be-comes determined to lash out with frustration and anger. Similarly, people sometimes commit to apathy and cyni-cism. If someone becomes convinced that change isn't pos-sible and others don't care about them, *they* decide not to care, no matter how much this undermines others or harms the organization. Perpetual doubt is a milder form of this. It's the cautious "wait-and-see" attitude that keeps com-mitment, and others, at arm's length.

Most of the time, people embrace conditional commitment. That is, they remain committed only as long as people and events meet their needs and expectations. But in a crisis, they remain ready to leave or give up and let failure happen. This is often true in business, but it can be equally true in romantic relationships, friendships, and even families.

Of course, wholehearted commitment is the highest, deepest form of commitment. This is the ideal of genuine caring, no matter what. We take responsibility for our words and actions, and we put aside our own expectations in order to meet people wherever they are. We want ourselves, our relationships, our team, and our workplace to succeed, and we commit to the group's or organization's shared vision and to overcoming any obstacle by turning breakdowns into breakthroughs.

If this is the level of commitment you desire, listening for understanding is the key for creating it. However, there are several other practices that can help cultivate this form of commitment:

Use "we," not "I": Listen to the language that you and others use to describe your relationship, organization, team, or project. If you frequently use "I, me, my," start saying "we, us, our." Shift the focus from egos and personalities to teams and shared efforts. Embody in your language that everyone is listening, learning, and succeeding together.

Talk about commitment: Explicitly value commitment, mutual respect, and honesty; acknowledge people for these things. Shift from emphasizing personal goals and achievements to company goals and achievements, and formally recognize accomplishments and good efforts with appreciation.

Schedule commitment meetings: Create times for people to share their doubts, concerns, needs, and goals. During these meetings, listen for understanding, and from them, develop shared commitments.

Don't get stuck in the past: It's easy to focus on what's gone wrong. Experiment with language as a way to shift from old habits: "In the past we may not have listened well. Now we aspire to be more present and caring." As I explain in the next chapters, listen for gaps with a sense of what's possible moving forward. Create a clear vision and focus on turning breakdowns into breakthroughs.

4

Mind the Gaps

The creative individual is particularly gifted in seeing the gap between what is and what could be.

— John W. Gardner

I've become a student of frustration. There is no shortage of events and situations to be frustrated about. There's gun violence, politics, and climate change, for a start. These are examples of enormous gaps between how things actually are and how we want them to be and know they could be.

Then there's our work and personal lives, where the gaps between what we are aiming for and what is are everywhere — from projected income to current income, from the forecasted progress at project launch to the actual progress and missed deadlines, from the type of relationships and culture we aspire to create to those we have. There can be gaps in how long we hoped it would take to solve a problem and in how long we hoped it would take to get from here to there. There can be gaps in the closeness of our relationships — with a partner, children, and parents.

There are always gaps in our personal development, since we aspire to be more aware, more skillful in working with conflicts, better able to express ourselves, more creative, more inspired.

There are even gaps in our efforts to close all these gaps between what we want and what is. Very little goes exactly as we might want it to, and if it ever does, that doesn't last long. This is the Buddha's first noble truth: There are gaps, gaps everywhere, and it will always be so.

To paraphrase Homer Simpson, why does life have to be so difficult, complicated, and disappointing?

Nevertheless, as our accountability expert, Homer has lots of advice for coping with the frustrating gaps that inevitably plague us. When things are not going the way his daughter, Lisa, wants in her work, he tells her: "Lisa, if you don't like your job, you don't go on strike. You just go in every day and do it really half-assed. That's the American way."

Homer also offers some terrific and actionable advice for dealing with perceptions of competence: "It's so simple to be wise ... Just think of something stupid to say and then don't say it."

And those can sometimes seem like our only choices: to give up and not do or say anything so we don't fail, or to just "do it really half-assed." Is it any wonder when we let anxiety rule, stop truly listening to others, and at best give our conditional commitment to any particular relationship or job?

There is another way, which is the practice I call "mind the gaps." In essence, this practice is one way to interpret and merge the Buddha's second and third noble truths:

Don't avoid gaps or the discomfort they cause; be curious about them, drop our stories, and listen more closely. While we can't avoid gaps and discomfort, we can still find skillful and effective ways to move closer toward the results we want. When we mind the gaps, we seek improvement, not perfection. We build healthy relationships, not idealized ones.

Working skillfully with gaps is another aspect of compassionate accountability. We have compassion for ourselves and others as we try to close the gaps, and this can greatly reduce frustration and anxiety and increase effectiveness, while accountability means noticing and not avoiding gaps. Through finding clarity, through listening for understanding, we recognize and acknowledge gaps and then confront them as best we can.

> When we mind the gaps, we seek improvement, not perfection. We build healthy relationships, not idealized ones.

How? As the Dodo advises Alice: "The best way to explain it is to do it."

Identifying Gaps: A 360-Degree View

One way to identify, better understand, and work skillfully with gaps in relationships is by doing a 360-degree review. In a corporate context, I've done many, probably hundreds, 360-degree performance reviews during my time as an executive coach. A 360-degree performance review is a process of interviewing a wide, diverse range of colleagues who work with the person I'm coaching — usually this includes people who work around, next to, above, and below the person (thus, 360 degrees). This might include their peers, people they report to, and those who report to them.

These reviews seek to identify gaps between the person's aspirations for being an effective leader and how they are perceived by those they work with. In the interviews, I ask people to describe what they want from this person as a leader, what they actually experience, and what they suggest the person do to become a more effective leader. All the feedback is then summarized and turned into a development plan to help the person to reduce or close the gaps, increase their effectiveness, and foster a mutually supportive, full-functioning team.

Below, I describe the process I use for business leaders, and then I explain how to adapt this to any circumstance, personal or professional. Typically, I ask six standard questions, and I find that these give me a tremendous amount of information in a relatively short time. I also find that this process in itself helps create a more supportive environment, with greater accountability, openness, and compassion. The underlying intention — to help the person improve their effectiveness — is an expression of care, and when done skillfully, the process creates greater transparency and understanding.

Here are the six core questions that make up a 360 interview:

1. What do you most appreciate about this person?
2. On a scale of 1 to 10, how would you rate this person's effectiveness as a leader? (10 is outstanding and 1 is terrible. No need to overthink the number; whatever comes to mind.)

3. Once I have the number, I ask: What would a 10 look like? What behaviors would this person need to do differently, to do more or less of, to be rated a 10? How can they close the gap between your rating and a 10?

4. What are other development issues that you think this person should address? Are there other gaps between your expectations and how you experience this person, such as in how they communicate in meetings and with team members?

5. What are *you* working on as a leader? What are some key elements of your development plan?

6. Is there anything else I should know that would help me in working with this person?

Appreciation

I think it's important to begin the interviews by focusing on appreciation. I want to set the tone that my intention is to look for strengths. It's also helpful to the person I'm working with to know all the ways that they are appreciated by their peers. I've interviewed executive teams that are in real conflict, where frustration and anger seem to dominate their relationships. Within these difficult emotions, I'm often surprised to hear the immense amount of appreciation these leaders have for one another. Of course, appreciation is a powerful antidote for anger and frustration. Appreciation alone can help pave the way toward closing gaps, and these interviews provide a sometimes rare opportunity to express it.

Accountability and Alignment

The next three questions focus on accountability and alignment. I probe for gaps and how to fix them. I'm almost always surprised how rarely people think in this way. This process helps people step back, reflect, and explore what's possible. The focus isn't really on problems but on what needs to shift or change to help transform those behaviors and gaps into possibilities. Simply naming gaps has a way of reducing the stories and emotions, particularly the discomfort and frustration, around the gaps.

Turning the Tables

With the fifth question, I turn the tables on the person I'm interviewing and ask them what they are working on in terms of leadership. This usually surprises the person. Everyone might assume that a 360-degree review is about the person in the middle, the executive I'm coaching, but it's really about cultivating a more-effective team. For everyone to work together in a supportive way, for everyone to embody compassionate accountability, everyone needs to be working on their personal and professional development. Accountability requires that we each are accountable for our emotions and how we communicate, and compassion requires that we move away from a mindset of blame, of pointing fingers at "those difficult people." Everyone involved is trying their best to be both compassionate and accountable.

The sixth question — an open-ended "Is there anything else?" — can elicit surprising and useful information. It's a way of addressing what really matters, what is most essential, and ways to work together more effectively.

· · ·

Following these interviews, I sift together all the responses and information and present it to the person I'm coaching. We use this to create more clarity and identify core gaps between what people experience and what they expect. Then we draft a development plan for closing or reducing those gaps.

After three months, I generally perform another round of interviews with a similar set of questions to see whether there are noticeable changes in behavior and observable reductions in the identified gaps. Depending on what's discovered, we adjust the development plan.

Doing Your Own 360-Degree Review

The principles and even the format of a professional 360-degree performance review can be adapted to various circumstances. In essence, finding more clarity and fostering compassionate accountability means being in a continual learning mode. It is an ongoing effort. This kind of review provides an opportunity to identify what's working well and where the gaps are and to develop a plan for improvement. But in order to keep everyone aligned and accountable, it's helpful to periodically reassess whether people are successfully cultivating the culture they desire and have agreed to.

You can mine the important lessons and usefulness of a 360 without a coach and without implementing a formal process. Simply have direct and open conversations with your colleagues, with the people who work for you and those you work for. You can do the same with family members, with friends or community groups, or with any important relationship (see "The Four Most Important Words" below).

Start with appreciation. Identify where there is alignment, where there aren't any gaps. Then bring curiosity to the question of what success looks like, both to you and others. Describe what you want in this relationship, situation, or group, and ask others to describe what they want. Have everyone envision what a 10 looks like in terms of working together, or other aspects of being together, and then consider what needs to be done to move toward or achieve that ideal.

Finally, either formally or informally, draft a development plan. Name what you and others will do differently so you can have a more effective relationship. Name examples and be specific. What do others want more or less of? What do you want more or less of? Implement those changes, and after a few months or so, talk to the people involved and reflect on what's better and what still needs improvement.

Survey the Company

Another way to assess your effectiveness as a leader, as well as to assess your organization as a whole, is to do an anonymous company survey. This can be given to everyone in the company or just to particular teams, divisions, or groups. And the survey can focus narrowly on a few key issues or be wide-ranging, addressing company culture, individual job satisfaction, work-group dynamics, management, compensation, and career development. In appendix 2, "Company Survey," I include a sample survey that is based on one I used when I was CEO of the Search Inside Yourself Leadership Institute. Adapt this to fit your needs and organization.

Feedback done anonymously can be enormously helpful, even when the responses are at times difficult to hear. Personally, I found it really painful to discover that not everyone in my organization loved me or thought I was a good leader. However, it was extremely important to learn that I needed to pay more attention to how I was impacting others, that I needed to address gaps in the personal and professional development of our employees. Further, the information gathered from this survey helped me identify specific, effective actions I could take to create a more compassionate and accountable work environment. I suggest doing such a survey at least once a year, maybe twice, and share the results with your staff, so everyone can design a development plan together.

The Four Most Important Words

To me, when it comes to the practice "mind the gaps," the four most important words are "How are we doing?"

Have you discovered the power of these four words? In a way, this question represents the simplest version of a 360-degree review. Sometimes, this is all that is needed to assess and explore the status of any relationship. "How are we doing?" can be used to launch a conversation with our partner, our children, our parents, our boss, our coworkers, our friends. These four words are a simple way to find clarity and embody compassionate accountability related to

> To me, when it comes to the practice "mind the gaps," the four most important words are "How are we doing?"

any aspect of our life, any role or goal we might have. Particularly with people we love, they are a means for exploring the quality of that love. We ask someone what, if anything, might improve the way we care for them.

How we ask this question makes a big difference in how it is answered and in the conversation that follows. Beforehand, assess how you feel, and acknowledge for yourself any fears, anxieties, doubts, judgments, or negative stories. Do you already think you know the answer, and so the question is more of a statement that you recognize something is missing, lacking, or wrong? Is the question really a prelude to a request for something *you* need from the other person?

Recognize and acknowledge whatever is true for you, but when you actually ask this question, try to let go of any negative stories and feelings. Ask in a spirit of genuine curiosity and openness. Be ready to listen for understanding to the other person's perspective and experiences, and be willing to be surprised. And remember, we convey this openness with our tone and body language as much as with our words. Does our voice and manner convey doubt, anxiety, or defensiveness, or do they convey caring, respect, and the willingness to have a genuine conversation? We can't pretend that fears don't exist, but we can also convey our core motivation to express caring in order to improve our connection. With these four words, we seek greater clarity to create better alignment, even when it's challenging.

Of course, how the other person responds will determine the conversation that follows, which may require a good deal of openness, presence, and skill. Our good intentions for asking the question are not enough. Our response to whatever the person says will require continued openness, trust, compassion, clarity, honesty, and integrity.

However, in the moment, our most important job is to listen. These four simple words express our willingness to recognize any gaps in our relationship and to be account-able for our words and actions. We ask because we care. We want to know the other person's experience and where they feel aligned and not aligned, and we want to know how they think we can eliminate or narrow any gaps. This inquiry in itself is an expression of our commitment to the relationship and our desire for it to embody shared values. These four words are an expression of compassion — of wanting to feel the other person's feelings, cultivate under-standing, and move toward greater healing.

Having Hard Conversations

My thirty-three-year-old daughter and I were on a walk together. We were on a trail just wide enough for us to be side-by-side in the hills of Missoula, Montana. My wife and I were visiting her, her husband, and their two-year-old son in their new home after they had spent the previous year and a half living in our home in Northern California. It was a clear, cold, crisp afternoon. As we walked, I could see snow-covered mountains to the north.

I had a strong feeling that my daughter had some re-sidual feelings of anger toward me and her mother. Several months earlier, during the time they were living with us, some serious miscommunication and misunderstandings had taken place. At that time, she had voiced that she was processing a lifetime of feelings, a lifetime of family dynamics she was frustrated with. At one point, she said she felt that her childhood role was to smooth out family difficulties to make it easier for her parents and her older brother. Now, as an adult and the mother of a young child, she wanted to change this pattern. She was working to heal her painful feelings from the past and transform them to improve her own well-being and create healthier family relationships.

We came to a place on the path that seemed like a natural stopping point. The views of the snow-covered mountains were spectacular. As we stopped, I turned to her and asked, "How are we doing?"

I wanted to better understand what she was thinking and feeling. In particular, I wanted more clarity about gaps — the differences in her experience and mine, and how we might find more alignment in our relationship.

I wanted to hear about her pain and dissatisfaction and how she perceived her role in our difficulties, and I wanted to apologize for the ways that I had contributed to past challenges. I wanted to express my deep love for her and make sure she knew I aspired for our relationship to be real, genuine. I wanted to move toward alignment as much as possible regarding what we wanted from each other.

Our conversation wasn't easy. I was surprised, and not, by the intensity of her feelings. I discovered that many of these negative feelings had nothing to do with me. She was feeling exhausted as a new mother. She was struggling through a major transition as they cultivated a new life in

Missoula. She and I have always had a deep and special connection, and she also wanted to rebuild our trust and create an easier, more loving connection.

I did a good deal of listening. I let her know what I was hearing. I expressed my deep intention to hear her feelings and her truth and for her to hear my feelings and my experience. And at the heart of it, I expressed my deep care, concern, and love.

It was an important conversation. My relationship with my children is important and meaningful to me beyond words. I came away with a deep sense of connection while knowing there was more work to do, more conversations to be had, more listening and understanding to cultivate.

The Urge to Avoid Gaps

Asking "How are we doing?" can sound easy, at least in theory, but noticing gaps in our relationships, whether in the workplace or in our families, can feel dangerous. It's uncomfortable to bring attention to our own feelings of vulnerability and discomfort and to acknowledge the signs, subtle or not-so-subtle, that there are problems and disconnects. Even when we believe that our relationships are working relatively well, we may feel an urge to avoid or deny gaps.

One reason is because denial and avoidance can feel safe and good! If no one is acknowledging problems, then we think, maybe there aren't any! Why rock the boat? If it ain't broke, don't fix it. Lots of Homer-esque wisdom sends the message that more trouble than good comes from asking about gaps and problems. Do we really want to know if things aren't going as well or as smoothly as we assume? By speaking up, might we open a can of worms and make things worse, create larger gaps, or harm our relationships? Or maybe we fear letting others see our own anger and frustration over gaps we know exist, and so we convince ourselves to let sleeping dogs lie. Or maybe we believe, based on past experience or previous conversations, that others don't care, won't listen, and have no interest in changing. If that's true, why bother? We'll only stir up a hornet's nest.

Watch out for these easy excuses and denials. See them for what they are: Red flags that you know or suspect that a problem exists. If so, be curious, investigate, explore, and see what you find. The problem might not be what you think, but if you continually pretend that everything is fine and no problems exist, you run the risk of losing the trust and respect of others.

On the other hand, another common experience is asking someone, "How are we doing?" and getting the reply "Fine" or "Everything's great!" Beware! Remember that everyone can be reluctant to acknowledge gaps, even when asked, even in otherwise trusting and excellent relationships. Do your best to cut through avoidance and denial. Persist. Sometimes a useful follow-up response to "fine" is: "I hope so, but I'm interested in what isn't fine. Is there anything I can do differently for our relationship to be better?"

Denial: When Positivity Creates Negativity

James is a publishing executive and member of his company's leadership team. As his executive coach, I did a 360-degree performance review for him, during which I discovered that several of his colleagues on the leadership team perceived James as deflecting problems. He tended to emphasize only what was working well and didn't engage with gnarly operational issues or address conflict among his key people. Invariably, James trumpeted his strengths and successes and covered over or ignored where his team experienced gaps, where people weren't in alignment, in addition to the places where he needed to grow and develop. As a result, his colleagues often didn't feel heard by James, who had become isolated and ineffective as a leader.

In this case, James's urge to give everything a positive spin was actually making things worse, and he needed to mind the gaps. I suggested that he speak to a number of key people he worked with — including members of his leadership team and the company's CEO — and ask for honest feedback. I suggested he voice his intention to be a 10 as a leader, and then to ask each person: "What can I do better or differently so that we can work together more effectively?"

A week later I received a note from Claire, a fellow member of the leadership team. She wrote, "What happened to James?" Then she expressed how surprised and pleased she was that he had asked for her feedback and then had just listened. Their conversation opened her eyes to things she had not been aware of, and they discussed an approach to dealing with issues that left her feeling like she could express more openly the challenges she was feeling every day. "Progress!" she said.

Both Claire and James recognized that this was just the first step in an ongoing process of improving their working relationship, but it was also a vivid example of how helpful and important honest conversations about gaps, goals, and alignment can be.

Pain Is Unavoidable, Frustration Is Extra

Recognizing and experiencing gaps can be painful. Not meeting our goals, targets, and expectations hurts. Being out of alignment hurts. And it hurts to acknowledge these things with the people we are out of alignment with. Then, it's easy to get stuck in feelings of stress, pain, and anxiety and to let these lead to frustration.

In addition to denial and avoidance, frustration is another danger to watch out for when it comes to working skillfully with gaps. In fact, to me, frustration and anxiety are a form of defensiveness. They can be a way of protecting ourselves from the discomfort of being let down or disappointed.

I recently facilitated a retreat of fifteen leaders of a manufacturing company. They had just completed a company-wide survey and were in a state of shock with how negatively their employees experienced the company culture. To illustrate this in a dramatic way, I created two word clouds. The word cloud for the ideal or desired culture featured words like *unified* and *supportive*, while in the word cloud for the current culture were words like *chaotic* and *dysfunctional*. As I flipped back and forth between these two word clouds, I asked the leaders how they felt. The room was filled with a good deal of discomfort and painful feelings.

"Frustration is extra," I suggested. "Of course, it's painful acknowledging these gaps. Let's not avoid these feelings, and let's find a path and a plan to create the culture you and your employees want. Let's shift, individually and as a team, from frustration to possibility."

Frustration can be debilitating. A mindset of frustration can seep into the water system, into the core underlying assumptions of individuals, teams, and cultures without it being clearly named or recognized. Frustration can become the way people relate and work together.

It's important to distinguish feelings of pain from feelings of frustration. Compassionate accountability does not mean avoiding or suppressing painful feelings. The compassion aspect of the practice is to keep our heart open, right in the midst of difficult situations. As Buddha suggested, we accept the pain rather than resist it. Then through accountability, we squarely face gaps and do whatever we can to address them.

In the leadership off-site, after I suggested that "frustration is extra," I brought up the topic of security. An essential quality for being able to work with gaps without frustration or resistance is feeling inner security. Inner security is a blend of confidence and humility — being confident in ourselves and our abilities and being willing to accept and understand our blind spots and to remain open to other perspectives.

This sense of inner security is something we can help foster in others through the practice of compassionate accountability. We do this through expressing genuine care, seeing others relationally and not just in their roles, and by minding the gaps so we are always making adjustments in how we communicate and work together. Airplane pilots don't become frustrated when they have to make course adjustments; that's to be expected in order to reach a destination thousands of miles away.

Another strategy for reducing frustration is to envision possible outcomes. Explore this practice. Imagine meeting your goals and expectations. Imagine what your relationships might look and feel like if you were more aligned, if you were able to reduce or close the gaps that exist. Ask others what their visions are. It can be potent and effective when everyone involved shares their visions of what is possible when everyone is working together at their best.

Negativity Bias: Assuming the Worst

It isn't just Homer Simpson. All humans exhibit a negativity bias. That is, we generally expect or assume the worst. This is another obstacle to watch out for with the practice of minding the gaps.

For instance, one common response to gaps, particularly when we give in to frustration, is to lower the bar. Instead of figuring out how to reach our goals and what we hope to achieve, we lower our expectations. Of course, particularly at work, some practical goals might be unrealistic and need revising; we may not be able to meet certain deadlines or make predicted sales goals. But in relationships, when it comes to how people work together, don't give in to lowering the bar on your aspirations. Since the tension of staying with gaps can feel uncomfortable and overwhelming, not settling for less can require a good deal of self-awareness and support.

Another danger that arises is our tendency to conflate a relatively minor conflict or disagreement into a much larger problem than it really is. Our emotions can run away from us, and having to admit to any gap at all can feel like a crisis, something that threatens our sense of self and confidence. Or conversely, others might feel unfairly criticized or that, by pointing out gaps, the intention is to put them down and humiliate them. These are forms of catastrophizing that obviously undermine our ability to fix gaps, so an important skill is to anticipate this and make it part of the conversation. For example, here are some ways to mitigate our negativity bias:

> "I appreciate that you feel safe and confident enough to disagree with me during meetings. Yesterday, though, I felt you were crossing the line from disagreeing to attacking."
>
> "I don't want you to think that I'm dissatisfied with how we work together. Sometimes, though, I'd like us to find ways to make decisions more quickly."
>
> "I can see how hard you are trying at school. I have some ideas that might help you in how you study for tests."

Even when gaps exist, they don't have to define our relationships or how we work together. We can include what's working well, and what success looks like, while directly and skillfully working with gaps.

The Truth Shall Make You Free

I once led a series of mindful leadership trainings just outside of Washington, DC, for business leaders and the CIA.

After going through multiple layers of security, as well as leaving all my electronic devices behind, I entered the CIA's main headquarters building. As I walked into the enormous, high-ceiling lobby, I looked up to read the inscription: *The Truth Shall Make You Free.*

The *truth* is that we tend to see ourselves and the world through the lens of our particular identities. Working with gaps is the work of searching for our truth and the truth of our relationships and situations. This search, this aspiration for alignment and accountability, means shifting from being caught by our limitations — by the patterns that don't serve us — and finding more emotional and existential freedom. This work involves becoming clearer about our stories, our emotions and mistaken beliefs, waking up to ways we limit ourselves and distort the truth, and living more in reality.

5

Cultivate a Clear Vision

*The function of a leader — the one universal requirement
of effective leadership — is to catalyze a clear and shared
vision of the organization and to secure commitment to
and vigorous pursuit of that vision.*

— Jim Collins and Jerry Porras, *Built to Last*

n a conversation with the Cheshire Cat, Alice gives us the
key to this practice:

"Would you tell me, please, which way I ought to
walk from here?"

"That depends a good deal on where you want
to get to," said the Cat.

"I don't much care where —" said Alice.

"Then it doesn't matter which way you walk,"
said the Cat.

"— so long as I get *somewhere*," Alice added as
an explanation.

"Oh, you're sure to do that," said the Cat, "if
you only walk long enough."

In other words, if you don't care where you go, you don't need to cultivate a clear vision. Just skip this chapter, keep walking, and you'll get somewhere. My guess, however, is that, unlike Alice, you actually want to get some place in particular. Maybe you don't know where that place is, or even what it is, but wandering aimlessly...just isn't very satisfying or effective.

To find your way, cultivating a clear vision is essential.

The Importance of Knowing Where You're Going

As an executive coach, I sometimes receive resistance or push back about the practice of envisioning. Many times, someone has protested, "I thought mindful leadership was about being in the present moment and not thinking about the future." Or someone will object, "I thought it was best to let go of our expectations."

Of course, in the moment, bringing awareness to that moment is important, as is letting go of holding on too tightly to outcomes. But that doesn't mean we don't imagine possible scenarios or plan, dream, and envision desired futures. Otherwise, it doesn't matter what we do, we can't lead or work with others effectively, and there's little to learn. We did something and got *somewhere*, but if we didn't aim for anything, we can't say whether we succeeded and we can't improve to do better next time. Not having a vision can be a self-defeating strategy for avoiding the discomfort of gaps.

Visions are powerful. They name the place we want to reach and the reason for what we are doing. A vision is a road map that defines success and how we imagine getting there. It is also a call to action that creates a sense of shared purpose and allows everyone involved to coordinate their efforts. Visions direct company strategy and guide the work of employees and departments so everyone is pulling in the same direction. When employees embrace a company's vision and the culture that creates, "the" company shifts to "our" company. A vision shapes our reality, our experience, and can change the world.

Visions ignite and unite. Visions bring our ideas to life and illuminate the path we seek. Visions bring people together to accomplish what we can't accomplish as individuals.

Developing a vision is itself a skill. People are often surprised when I present developing and expressing a vision as a competency, something that can be learned, practiced, developed, and honed. For instance, a successful vision provides a means for cultivating compassionate accountability. Implementing a vision involves measuring, testing, and evaluating progress. It provides a framework for groups to assess how well they are working together, and it allows everyone to track progress and make adjustments along the way. Everything is always changing — people, environments, markets, society — and a clear vision can help us shift and adapt when necessary and still reach our goals.

Cultivating a clear, credible, and inspiring vision requires a unique blend of passion, artistry, and imagination. It requires curiosity and is supported by deep listening. A vision can help cut through the frustration of gaps and

> Cultivating a clear, credible, and inspiring vision requires a unique blend of passion, artistry, and imagination. It requires curiosity and is supported by deep listening.

transform those gaps into stories of possibility, clarity, and success.

A Vision Starts with Values

When asked by the Cheshire Cat, Alice is unable to say where she wants to go, but that doesn't mean she doesn't care. Developing a vision starts with being aware of and articulating what we care about in the grand scheme of things. We name our core values. Individuals, teams, companies, and families are all guided by their values, whether those are stated or unstated. Visions embody what is most important to us, which reflects our sense of self, our life experience, and our aspirations. Our core values define what we stand for, and a vision statement expresses our core values, important beliefs, and intrinsic principles in a way that names what we hope to achieve and guides our decisions about how to accomplish those things and how to work together.

Here is a list of values that are often cited by leaders and people I work with:

Accountability, trust, diversity, honesty, curiosity, boldness, inclusion, humility, integrity, making a difference, courage, simplicity, vulnerability, patience, competence

For yourself, write down the values that matter to you most. These will eventually form the core of your vision statement. As a way to help consider and articulate your values, I've found the following journaling exercise to be surprisingly effective:

1. Write down the names of three people you most admire. These can be anyone living or dead, famous or not famous. They can be family members, movie characters, or mythological people. Let yourself be surprised by whoever comes to mind.

2. Once you've chosen these three people, write down next to each person's name why you chose them. What did they do or represent? This can be a single accomplishment or many; it could be how they lived, who they helped, or what qualities they embody. Let your intuition guide you, and write as much or as little as you want.

3. The people we most admire typically represent the values we most care about and want to embody in our own way. Distill what you wrote about others into your top values. This might be one single value, but I encourage people to write down at least two or three, but no more than five. The point is to distill what is most important to us, not to include everything we value.

You can use this same exercise when creating a shared vision statement with a group. Simply have everyone do this on their own and then share the three people they chose and the values they came up with.

Another effective way to explore your values is to imagine what you want to accomplish, either at work or in your life overall. Travel into the future and imagine that you've done whatever that is. If you wish, treat this as a journaling prompt, giving yourself seven to twelve minutes to write, or simply think about it. What might your life look like if everything went in alignment with your highest hopes? How would you feel, what would you be doing, and what current problems would you have solved? Now consider what values this success represents or embodies. Again, distill that into a list of two to five values.

Mission and Vision: What Brings You Here?

I often begin leadership trainings and workshops with two questions designed to clarify intentions and personal vision. The first question is:

What brings you here?

The second question is:

What really brings you here?

Like the Cheshire Cat, I want people to name where they want to go, their destination. The first question is about naming what's most important in this moment. I'm encouraging people to ask: *What am I seeking to accomplish in this workshop? What is my vision of a successful use of our time together in this room?*

The second question asks them to articulate their larger, even existential goals: *What brings me to this profession, to this life?* I want participants to look more deeply and name their values. I want to cut through the usual business speak, which is all about analysis and action, and have people speak from their hearts, to get real. I want them to name their vision.

People sometimes attend workshops or trainings because their boss told them to, or they want to pick up some leadership tools to use at work. Those motivations emerge in the answer to the first question. But to answer the second question, we acknowledge and articulate more profound and universal intentions. We name the aspirations that often exist beneath the surface and give meaning to everything we do. These are the motivations that guide us as we navigate our work and personal lives, as we make choices and take action even in the midst of uncertainty.

Like Alice, we don't always know what these values are. Maybe we avoid thinking about them out of fear, or maybe we have just never stopped to ask ourselves this question. It can be easier to stay on the surface, to focus on what we're doing and not on why. Another way to characterize this is the difference between mission and vision. In business, these terms are often used interchangeably or combined into the same statement. But traditionally, mission defines the organization's purpose in terms of what it plans to do and accomplish. Vision describes why that is important; it articulates where the organization aspires to go and the impact it wants to have.

You might pause right now and ask yourself these two questions:

1. What brings you here?
2. What really brings you here?

You can define "here" in several different ways. Why are you here reading this book? Why are you with your partner or family? Why are you in your job or with your company? Why are you in your profession? Or step further back and ask: Why are you alive, here and now, on this planet? Perhaps in your journal, consider every major arena in your life and ask: What brings you here, and what really brings you here? Creating a vision begins by looking with curiosity underneath the surface of everyday life in order to see and feel more deeply.

Writing a Personal Vision Statement

Once you've articulated your values and explored these two questions — that is, named your reasons for being here — draft a personal vision statement that captures the larger, deeper aspirations for your life. This is like a statement of purpose that directs your life energy and names where you want to go. In a sentence or two, write a vision statement that expresses what is most important to you. In fact, you might find it helpful to draft several vision statements for different arenas of your life: for your personal life goals, and for your family, work, and spiritual practice.

Here are some examples of personal vision statements:

- I aspire to develop and use my writing skills to inspire and educate others to make sustainable social change.
- I want to be a lifelong learner who cultivates a sense of wonder.
- I want to help adults and children find meaning and hope after significant loss.
- I aspire to help reduce bias and racism in my community and the world.
- I aim to create a future where expectant mothers have the support and resources needed to thrive.

- I want to approach my job as an arena for growth and learning and to foster compassionate accountability in my workplace.

Many Plans, One Shared Vision

Just as each of us as individuals can be more effective if we name our personal vision for our lives, every group, family, team, company, and corporation can articulate a shared vision that embodies what the group values, that names its purpose and what it is striving for. What can happen when this is lacking was driven home to me during a recent two-day workshop retreat with twelve leaders of a midsize financial services company. We were just beginning the second day, and the topic for the morning was the "elephants in the room." I wanted everyone to name the issues that they found the most difficult and dangerous to talk about, or whatever important issues had been ignored or avoided for some time. There was a good deal of energy around this particular exercise. I asked everyone to write down their top three "elephants" on a piece of paper, and then pass them to me at the front of the room.

> Just as each of us as individuals can be more effective if we name our personal vision for our lives, every group, family, team, company, and corporation can articulate a shared vision that embodies what the group values.

Right away, even before we launched into addressing these issues, Maria, the senior vice president of operations, raised her hand and stated, with some emotion and frustration, "We don't have a plan." Around the room, I could see and feel strong reactions to this statement. There were many nods of agreement and some looks of discomfort, disbelief, and disagreement.

Marty, the company's chief financial officer, chimed in right away. "Of course we have a plan," he said. "We know exactly what the financial projections are, revenue and expenses, for each area of the organization." Ronnie, the head of marketing, jumped in and asserted, "Of course we have a plan. We have a three-year strategic plan, approved by the board. You all have this strategy document. It's in all your inboxes."

The statement "We don't have a plan" was being received by some as provocative or blaming. I suggested that Maria restate her assertion as: "*I* don't feel we have a plan. I feel a sense of frustration and worry." This way, Maria's statement became a description of her experience, not necessarily a statement of fact. Reframed in this way, there was a good deal less defensiveness and more curiosity in the room.

In groups, when we speak from our own experience, when we use "I" statements, we take responsibility for our perspective; we express accountability. This creates a greater sense of safety within the group, since it avoids others feeling like they are being criticized by implication. This allows for more listening, more understanding, and better connection.

I asked Maria if her operations team had a plan. She said, "Yes, of course operations has a plan. What I mean is that I don't see how our departments work together. I don't know the plan for our company. Each area within the company has a plan, but I don't understand how they fit together."

This organization, like most, had a financial plan and a strategic plan. Each of the twelve executives sitting in the room, the top leaders in their organization, had individual plans for their own departments, but there wasn't a clear shared vision for the company itself — a statement of purpose that they had all agreed on and could rally around, one that named their values and guiding principles, their mission and why they existed, which would allow them to coordinate their efforts and achieve what they were aiming for in the world.

The Power of a Shared Vision

A shared vision is like letting the genie out of the bottle. It becomes more than an idea, more than a vision. It connects people's minds and hearts. It provides a guide and a direction that people want to align with and be part of, want to commit to and work toward together. It creates and supports an environment of connection and possibility. We do things together — work long and hard hours, practice a skill or a sport, do seven- and ten-day meditation retreats, or build thriving organizations — that we could not do without a compelling shared vision.

Caring may be one of the most powerful forces on Earth. A shared vision taps into what we already care about and makes it clearer, stronger, moving us toward taking action. A vision might open our worlds to something new, an idea that we had never considered, something we had never thought of before.

A clear shared vision is inspiring and surprising. It lands in our hearts like the language that the Boeing executive recognized in the poetry of David Whyte. A vision that's worth committing to may be simple or bold, quiet or loud, but it opens the doorway of what's possible to bring about life-altering positive change.

Creating a Shared Vision Statement

Any group or organization might be described as a vision in action. A company might start as a single person's idea, but eventually and inevitably it becomes a shared idea, and as this happens, as it is embraced by a community or group, the vision develops and morphs. For visions to successfully take root, whether in organizations or families, those involved need a sense of "buy-in" — a feeling of shared ownership. The vision must matter to many, so it moves from "your vision" or "their vision" to "our vision."

When creating a shared vision, the aspiration is to name a clear common goal, whatever you are hoping to achieve together, along with a sense of how you aspire to get there and of what matters most to your shared work as a group. When creating a shared vision, whatever type of group it is — whether a family, team, or company — aim for the process to incorporate these four aspects:

Engagement: Maybe it goes without saying, but an effective shared vision includes the input and involvement of everyone (or at least most) in the group. Organize the process so that as many people as possible have a say, are heard, and make a contribution. Seek to embody the classic text by Lao-tzu in the Tao Te Ching:

A leader is best
When people barely know he exists.
Of a good leader, who talks little,
When his work is done, his aim fulfilled,
They will say, "We did this ourselves."

Heart: An effective vision is clear, actionable, and evokes strong, heartfelt emotions.

Alignment: In a group, work toward alignment, so that most people agree. This is an ongoing process of involvement and empowerment.

Flexibility: In groups, it's easy to go down the rabbit hole of working to get every word just right. Don't get stuck on wordsmithing. Perfection can be the enemy of the good.

A Family Vision Statement

Most families cultivate shared values, but they don't usually have a shared vision statement. Why is that? Is it too obvious, too hokey, too difficult? Creating a family vision statement can help define what really matters to your family and provide guidance for how you want family members to treat one another and work together.

Talking about values is the place to begin. Values might include honesty, generosity, compassion, service, humor, learning, appreciation, and integrity. Ask each family member what they value, and explore ranking or prioritizing these values. What values are shared by all? Which are considered most important? Then, as a family, embody this in some creative way. It doesn't need to be a written statement;

it could be a poem, a photo, a painting, or a collage. Rather than hold formal "meetings," this conversation could be conducted informally over several meals.

Here are some ideas for how a family vision statement might read:

- We appreciate each other and feel gratitude for all that we have.
- We support each other and work together as a team.
- We embrace compassion, accountability, and vulnerability.
- We address conflicts and breakdowns with care and understanding.
- We are each learning and growing, and we support our individual and family development.
- We aspire to make the world a better place.

Once you have a family vision statement, post it somewhere visible. Refer to it from time to time, and change and update it as needed. See what works and what could be improved. Notice the gaps between what is and your aspirations, and address openly how you can work together to close those gaps.

A Company Vision Statement

A vision statement is typically a future-focused concept that evokes the impact you want your company to have in the world. It's an idealized expression of the kind of world your values embody, or the larger purpose of your company's existence. A company *mission* statement is often more concrete and detailed. It might describe the specific ways your company is working to make your vision a reality. In addition, the mission statement often distinguishes your company from others in the same space or field, or that have similar aspirations. The focus here is primarily on the importance and effectiveness of having a clear vision.

Forming and expressing a clear vision involves deep listening and ongoing conversations that explore "What does success look like?" and "How are we doing?" Leadership needs to work toward aligning around a clear, credible, and measurable vision, and then communicating that vision to teams and the entire organization.

A company vision statement isn't just for leadership or the CEO. It's for customers, employees, and all stakeholders. It describes the kind of culture you aspire to create and sets the direction of the company, naming the aspirational goals you are working together to achieve. People may keep this in mind when deciding whether to do business with you or whether to work for you. It can help employees see and understand how their day-to-day work connects to and supports the larger vision, and it can motivate and inspire employees to generate new ideas that align with the vision.

Here are a few examples of company vision statements:

- Kiva: To expand financial access to help underserved communities thrive.
- Asana: To help humanity thrive by enabling all teams to work together effortlessly.
- Nike: Bring inspiration and innovation to every athlete in the world. (If you have a body, you are an athlete.)

- Patagonia: Build the best product, cause no unnecessary harm, use business to inspire and implement solutions to the environmental crisis.
- LinkedIn: Create economic opportunity for every member of the global workforce.
- Zoom: Video communications empowering people to accomplish more.

Strong Visions Create a Collaborative Culture

A strong, clear vision is an important aspect of cultivating greater collaboration, and it's the ground of accountability. It helps track both results and process. This is where collaboration becomes particularly interesting and leads to surprising results, especially in the realm of teams. When a team is not aligned, there can be a tremendous amount of apathy, wasted energy, conflict, and ineffectiveness. When a team is working and learning together, the collective insights, skills, creativity, and wisdom of the team can be vastly higher than any individual. The core practices for effective team learning are shared optimism, suspending judgment, focus and flexibility, and asking unexpected questions, which are core elements of compassionate accountability.

Shared optimism: An individual harboring a positive belief is a powerful force. A team working together with a shared sense of optimism and belief in their purpose, creativity, and effectiveness is that force multiplied.

Suspending judgment: Learning together means putting aside individual negativity bias and the inner critic, which can easily and seamlessly appear and hamper the possibility of real curiosity, listening, and learning. When criticisms and judgments arise, recognize them and, if possible, meet them with humor and friendliness.

Focus and flexibility: High-functioning teams tend to be highly focused and flexible. They deeply explore issues, viewpoints, ideas, and solutions. They enter meetings fully prepared, and they focus on driving toward solutions and outcomes and developing action plans to meet their shared vision. At the same time, they are open to new ideas, patterns, and possibilities. They know they need to be flexible and ready to move in creative and surprising new directions.

Unexpected questions: Teams learn and grow together when they remain open to asking and grappling with unexpected questions. They look at problems and solutions from a variety of perspectives, and team members feel safe to question processes and assumptions. Everyone understands that supporting the team's creative process means there are no "dumb" questions.

• • •

A high-functioning team, family, or group — one that is learning and working together — can resemble a jazz group, riffing off each other, influencing and enjoying each person's contribution and creating an outcome that is pleasing and at times magical. Like a jazz group, there can be individual performances, where each person has a chance to shine, but the priority is for the team as a whole to shine, formulating and expressing their shared vision.

6

Turn Breakdowns into Breakthroughs

The ground where you stumble and fall is the same ground
you use to stand up.

— Shunryu Suzuki

A central practice in implementing compassionate accountability is our view and response to breakdowns, challenges, difficulties, and failures. It's the breakdowns and how we engage with and learn from gaps, failures, and misalignments — the ones that surprise us and test us — that often provide the ground for growth and learning.

Ideally, in one way or another, we set the intention to do many of the practices the book has suggested so far. We do the inner work to find clarity within ourselves — by being curious, dropping our story, and cultivating an aspirational vision for our lives that reflects our core values. We work with others to untangle the tangles, listen with understanding, and mind any gaps we discover. We practice compassionate accountability and develop shared visions that aim to create caring relationships and effective, mutually supportive, high-functioning teams that know how to work together to accomplish common goals. We do this in our work life and our personal and family lives, seeking to foster trusting connections where everyone feels safe to be open and honest. As much as we can, we try to put everything in place in order to succeed.

Then, life happens. We are surprised by unexpected consequences. Others don't live up to our visions and aspirations. We don't live up to our own visions and aspirations. Perhaps we unintentionally upset a coworker or a friend. Or someone lets us down, despite their promises to change habits and do better. Perhaps the accounting department keeps missing important deadlines. Or children lie about where they've been or why they aren't completing schoolwork, which can't be because the dog finds it delicious. Perhaps we turn away from or ignore gaps and warning signs. We promise to attend to problems soon and realize we've waited too long when a key employee enters our office to resign. Despite our best intentions and well-designed practices, situations and relationships can go sideways or completely off the rails.

> It's the breakdowns and how we engage with and learn from gaps, failures, and misalignments — the ones that surprise us and test us — that often provide the ground for growth and learning.

That's what this chapter discusses: how to acknowledge, work with, and transform these breakdowns into breakthroughs. Breakdowns will occur despite our best intentions, but turning them into breakthroughs is a core aspect of finding clarity and compassionate accountability.

Are You Cynical or Are You Engaged?

It is very common to feel that we lack influence with other people and are powerless to enact change. Feeling powerless can lead to cynicism and a sense of victimhood. Cynicism is a belief and attitude that people only act from their self-interest and that change is impossible. Once feelings of victimhood and cynicism take hold in organizations or in important relationships, they can block addressing and working effectively with the many challenges of working together, of misalignments and breakdowns.

The antidote to feeling powerless is to adopt the perspective of engagement. When engaged — even while recognizing that, as Homer so aptly states, "everything is so *hard*" — we understand that problems are not immovable. A key insight is distinguishing between events and how we interpret and respond to those events. We are engaged when we live, breathe, and act from this distinction. This helps us let go of blame and accept responsibility for changing our situation.

We can always influence our attitude, our viewpoint, and our approach to difficulties, challenges, and breakdowns. When we feel powerless, we make ourselves victims of circumstance. We get stuck in a narrow view of ourselves and are unable to envision change or success.

When we adopt the perspective of engagement, we see more clearly and face difficulties and challenges with a solution-focused mindset, even when everything looks challenging and at times impossible. It's not that we never again slip into a cynical mentality, but we recognize it as an opportunity to shift approaches and become more positive and optimistic.

Notice Your Own Avoidance

One of the most important things to notice is avoidance. As the Buddha advised: There is no avoiding pain, suffering, and breakdowns. They are an inevitable part of life. So the first and most important strategy for dealing with them is to not be too surprised when they happen, even if we can't predict exactly what will go wrong. Simply face the problem, recognize the gap, and get to work.

However, it's equally important to remember that we all have an inner Homer. That is, we're only human, and at times, it's equally inevitable that we will try to avoid bad news. We will pretend not to see trouble or we will sidestep conflicts. We might pass the buck or hope breakdowns will just go away. Notice when avoidance arises — when you say or think what Homer once told his daughter:

> Lisa, I want to share something with you. The three little sentences that will get you through life: Cover for me. Oh, good idea. It was like that when I got here.

COVER FOR ME

We may not be quite so coarse as to openly say, "Cover for me," but how often do people not attend meetings in which others are counting on them? Or ask others to complete vital work that is their responsibility? In families, "cover for me" might show up as not fulfilling basic commitments like washing the dishes or cleaning the bathroom, on the assumption that someone else will notice and take care of it. These behaviors are generally a sign that either

(1) accountability and commitments are not taken seriously, (2) there is a level of disengagement that needs to be recognized, or (3) there is a more serious disconnect in a relationship.

In any case, notice when you or others are not living up to promises or expectations. See this as a sign of a problem, a misalignment, or a lack of trust and accountability.

OH, GOOD IDEA

Homer's second piece of advice is to agree with what others say, whether we truly agree with it or not. Homer is quite fond of this approach, once advising, "Never say anything unless you're sure everyone feels exactly the same way you do." False agreement is a popular strategy for avoiding conflict. It can also be a sign that basic safety is lacking. This arises when the environment in a relationship or group seems too dangerous to voice doubts or disagreements or to express alarm when decisions seem unwise or risky.

To address this in leadership trainings, I often ask people two questions:

How many of you say yes when you mean no?
How many of you avoid a conflict or difficult conversation by just moving on?

There is a good deal of squirming and many raised hands in response to these questions. Agreeing as a way to avoid conflict may work in the short term, but when it becomes a habit, it erodes trust, connection, and effectiveness.

It Was Like That When I Got Here

In company cultures that lack accountability, I often hear a common refrain: "It's always been like that here." What people mean is, nothing ever changes, so it's no use trying. When this cynical attitude or mindset infects a group or relationship, no one believes change is possible, and no matter what the problem, no one attempts to improve or fix it. Everyone just leaves the mess the way it is. They adopt the convenient excuse that, since they didn't make it, they shouldn't be the ones to clean it up. After all, "It was like that when I got here." In a way, this type of avoidance turns a lack of accountability into a virtue.

Safety First

Psychological safety is a term that has become increasingly common in the business world. First introduced at Harvard by Amy Edmondson, it became more well known as a result of a study that was conducted by Google called Project Aristotle. This was done to better understand why some teams are more effective than others. The surprising finding of this study was that psychological safety was the key element in high-performing, effective teams.

Psychological safety means creating an environment where people feel respected and cared about; where making mistakes is seen as part of learning; and where we see and want the best for others, and others see and want the best for us. We trust that others will not undermine us, and we pledge not to undermine them. A psychologically safe environment is open, authentic, and supportive; it allows everyone to try new things, experiment, take risks, and ask for help. In other words, in this environment, we anticipate, expect, and accept breakdowns, and we know that by turning them into breakthroughs, we will learn how to work more successfully and effectively together.

Without psychological safety, finding solutions becomes highly unlikely. Creating this sense of safety starts with genuine listening, but it often takes more than that.

As one of my mentors was fond of saying, as a leader, "everything you say and everything that you don't say, and everything that you do and everything that you don't do, has influence."

There are three key ingredients for creating an environment of psychological safety, whether at work, home, or any place:

- **Cultivate self-awareness:** Start with your own deep feelings of being safe. Calm your inner critic and awaken your aspiration to be curious about yourself — and to care for and love yourself — as much as possible.
- **Plan for success:** Define clear ground rules for creating an environment of compassionate accountability, where results and care for people both matter, and where mistakes and failures are part of learning.
- **Mind the gaps:** Acknowledge gaps, breakdowns, and failures. Celebrate successes, and model listening, confidence, and humility.

Walter: Minding the Gaps, Asking for Help

I had the opportunity to work with Walter, the CEO of a large manufacturing company, and his leadership team to explore creating greater psychological safety. Though Walter's intention was to create a more caring and open work environment, he was quick to be critical of his direct reports and to provide solutions without much listening or collaboration. As a result, in his company, there was a good deal of accountability, but little compassion, and this had created a culture of fear.

In my one-on-one meetings with Walter and his team, we each discussed being more curious, listening more deeply, dropping stories, noticing mistaken beliefs, and working more skillfully with gaps. The core underlying work with Walter, his leadership team, and the organization was to cultivate more psychological safety as a means toward creating a more compassionate culture.

I then scheduled a luncheon with Walter and his six leaders. They were accustomed to Walter sitting at the head of the table and leading meetings, with little or no room for personal connection. As our lunch meeting began, I stood next to Walter and put my arm on his shoulder as I looked around the table and addressed the leaders. I said, "I know how scary Walter is. He can be a really terrifying guy. He knows this. He doesn't want to be and he needs your help. He wants each of you to continue to do great work, to feel more secure, and to be able to speak more openly and truthfully about what you see, feel, and need for this to be a more effective team."

This certainly got their attention. I felt some nervousness and a strong sense of relief and possibility in the room. Then

Walter spoke, and in his own words, he expressed that he wanted to create a team and culture of compassionate accountability and needed their help. Then each leader had a turn to respond. In their own ways, they each expressed their appreciation, some fears and concerns, and a commitment to be more present and to take more risks. This was the starting point for transforming their breakdown into a breakthrough.

Strategies for Approaching Breakdowns

In *The Splendid and the Vile,* author Erik Larson describes how during one of the most intense and dramatic periods of World War II, Winston Churchill acted with a remarkable sense of focus and flexibility, as well as with compassion and accountability. This was during a radically challenging time, when London was being attacked and destroyed by German firebombing. Churchill's approach provides useful and actionable lessons for turning breakdowns into breakthroughs. He focused on three things that build on what we've discussed so far:

- Purpose and meaning
- Cautious optimism
- No sugarcoating

Purpose and Meaning

Purpose and meaning relate to naming values and creating a shared vision of where you're going and why. When conflicts, difficulties, and breakdowns occur, one method for transforming them is to refocus everyone on the group's larger purpose. This might mean redefining what you are doing, who you are benefiting, and how you are serving them. Address your core values, what matters to you most, and ensure that how you are working together reflects this. In addition to the end result, focus on the kind of culture you are committed to creating and the kind of relationships you want to have and develop — with each other, with customers, with stakeholders, and with the world.

Remembering and perhaps redefining the group's core motivation, its purpose and meaning, can have a tremendous positive impact. Simply by not turning away from and addressing breakdowns, you help everyone access and draw strength from their larger purpose.

I experienced my share of breakdowns during my years as CEO of the Search Inside Yourself Leadership Institute. There were some serious conflicts and misalignments around strategy, some instances of employees not feeling seen or feeling safe, and a number of customer relationships and partnerships that fell apart as a result of miscommunications and differences in expectations. I always found it useful to return to our core purpose: Enlightened leaders worldwide, especially during these difficult situations. We existed in order to train leaders and individuals to be more aware and more effective, to have a positive influence in their organizations and beyond, and this included ourselves.

Cautious Optimism

Fostering cautious optimism in a group is often the result of creating a culture of psychological safety. That is, the world can be challenging, and problems can be daunting and dangerous, but if people feel safe within the group, they are more prone to cautious optimism as opposed to cynicism and victimhood. Optimism is important for meeting breakdowns: It can help us see more clearly and act more decisively, with all stakeholders in mind. Cautious optimism is not avoidance, or pretending problems don't exist or aren't serious; it's a form of courageous engagement that helps us work skillfully during difficult times.

Of course, this can be easier said than done. As I've noted, we humans have an inherent negativity bias; we are wired to imagine all the things that can go wrong or get worse. When emotions are high and we feel personally threatened and vulnerable, it's natural to feel defensive. Rather than face conflicts, our first impulse can be to deny trouble exists or to avoid it at all costs.

When fear or pessimism arises, imagine facing the breakdown and visualize what might go well. Then imagine what might happen if you ignore or avoid whatever the trouble is. Cautious optimism is the antidote to our negativity bias and it opens the door to possible positive outcomes — more trust, greater alignment, a more-effective team. Cautious optimism arises when we work together to find solutions within a culture that is open, direct, and caring.

No Sugarcoating

Finally, when facing and confronting breakdowns in themselves, foster an attitude of "no sugarcoating." Empower people to see clearly and tell it like it is. This is part of accountability, the ability to be honest about what we think the problems are. In order to effectively address breakdowns, we have to recognize them. Of course, this is more than a declaration. In a group or relationship, it means having a discussion in which everyone provides their perspective, and the group comes to an agreement about the nature of the breakdown and how to fix it.

Here are some of the practices that go into no sugar-coating:

- **Confront your reality:** See and feel what is happening with as much clarity as possible.
- **Befriend your fear:** Notice and engage with your fear and the impulse to avoid or attack.
- **Call upon your courage:** By cultivating a sense of inner safety, you help inspire the courage to face fear.
- **See difficulty as an opportunity:** Be fully in the moment, especially when it's painful and difficult. Look for opportunities to learn and grow, as well as to explore new and creative options.

Practicing Accountability

I once facilitated an off-site retreat for a leadership team of lawyers. One of the issues that emerged was that Sam, a senior attorney who happened to be a significant revenue earner for the company, was a terrible team player. He often snapped, yelled, and berated his fellow lawyers. Yet because Sam brought in significant revenue to the firm, his bad behavior had long been ignored or excused. Now several excellent long-term lawyers had communicated that they were planning to leave the company, in part due to Sam's bad behavior.

What to do? By avoiding the problem when it first started, the firm had let it grow to a genuine breakdown, yet they didn't want to lose Sam or the other lawyers. My advice was to have an accountability discussion with Sam, one with "no sugarcoating." Beware of the "Oreo cookie" approach to having difficult conversations. That is, when bad behavior or breakdowns are serious and openly acknowledged, don't begin with a compliment or positive small talk. Don't hide the problem in the middle, surrounding it with niceties.

There is a practice from Zen called "trust your own eyes." It's tempting to think that "compassionate accountability" means that we must always be "nice" or hold our emotions in check. Instead, I would make a case that mindfulness practice, and the practice of compassionate accountability, means being more real and more clear, to act with greater emotional freedom and honesty. When we feel hurt, be hurt. When angry, be angry. When differences of perspectives, violated expectations, or bad behaviors occur, we can see them clearly, feel them deeply, and act effectively — by insisting on accountability and focusing each person on the group's larger purpose. The keys are clarity and choice — to see and feel with as much clarity as possible, and to avoid reactivity and choose the most effective and appropriate response.

The practices in this book are not meant to be protections or shields from experiencing pain or from having our heart broken. In fact, compassion literally means to suffer with others. Compassionate accountability is not about minimizing or turning away from challenges and pain, but recognizing these as they arise. For instance, if you've asked people to arrive on time, and they are late, that is a problem that needs addressing. If you learn that some people at work are being talked about or treated in negative, demeaning, or inappropriate ways, this is a problem that needs addressing. Trust your own eyes. Don't sugarcoat. Face problems and conflicts as directly, compassionately, and effectively as possible.

> Compassionate accountability is not about minimizing or turning away from challenges and pain, but recognizing these as they arise.

When the time comes for an accountability discussion, plan ahead what you will say and how you will begin the conversation, particularly the first minute or so. Consider how you will present the problem, what you think are the best options for addressing it, and the consequences if the person doesn't agree and won't fix the problem or change their behavior.

As an example, here is how the conversation with Sam might start:

> Sam, I want to speak with you about a problem. We hear from several of our best attorneys that you have been yelling and demeaning others. Several attorneys are talking about leaving the company as a result of your actions. This is unacceptable. We value your work for the firm, but we need you to address this problem and change this behavior. Do you agree that this is a problem, and how do you propose fixing it?

From here, how the conversation goes depends on how Sam responds, on whether he agrees with the assessment of the problem and offers genuine solutions. Sam may have a different perspective. Of course, if Sam doesn't help resolve the problem in the way the firm wants, this might lead to a series of conversations and an escalation of consequences.

Clearings: Repairing Relationships

Sometimes, despite our best efforts, breakdowns in working relationships can erode to the point where there doesn't seem to be any hope of resolution. This is particularly challenging when the conflict or breakdown is between leaders or people working together on a team. These kinds of conflicts can happen at all levels of the workplace, with family members, and with friendships.

Clearings are a process to explore when two people have been unable to resolve a conflict or a serious misalignment, and there is a need and willingness to continue working together. The intended outcome of this process is to open a door to greater understanding. During clearings, both individuals intend to find a way to let go of blame, resentment, and whatever story they might be holding on to that is preventing them from working together cooperatively.

Initiating a Clearing

Typically, one person is the initiator. After expressing their positive intention to improve the relationship, they ask the other person if they are willing to engage in a clearing process.

If the other person agrees, the initiator shares their story of what happened. This should be done using "I" statements (see "Many Plans, One Shared Vision," page 117) and by acknowledging that this is their interpretation or understanding of events (see "The Story I'm Telling My-self Is ...," page 67, for more on this).

The initiator then describes how they have contributed to creating this disconnection. This should involve a genu-ine, not a token, acceptance of mutual responsibility for the problem.

Finally, this person should express what they hope for from this process, describing what they want from the other person and what they hope for in this relationship.

Listening and Responding During a Clearing

While the initiator talks, the other person should listen for understanding without interrupting. When the first person is finished, the listener describes the gist of what they heard the first person say. That is, the listener reiterates the other person's perspective in order to confirm that they have heard correctly.

Then, the two people change roles and repeat the pro-cess. The listener gets their turn to describe the story of what happened from their perspective, how they feel they contributed to the breakdown, and what they want from the other person and hope for in the relationship.

Ideally, this process will lead to some level of agree-ment about what happened and what to do next. However, it doesn't need to. The essential goal is for both people to listen to each other respectfully. In the end, each person should express how they've been influenced by this clear-ing process.

• • •

This discussion of breakdowns, failures, misalignments, and mistakes makes me think of a few lines from a poem by the Spanish poet Antonio Machado called "Last Night as I Was Sleeping":

> Last night as I was sleeping
> I dreamt — marvelous error! —
> that I had a beehive
> here inside my heart.
> And the golden bees
> were making white combs
> and sweet honey
> from my old failures.

Marvelous mistakes. Marvelous misalignments. Marvelous conflicts. All have the potential to be transformed. Maybe not always into sweet honey, but into opportunities for growth and learning, for greater accountability integrated with compassion.

7

Don't Wait

When it's over, I want to say: all my life
I was a bride married to amazement.
I was the bridegroom, taking the world into my arms.

— Mary Oliver, "When Death Comes"

Being curious, dropping the story, and listening for understanding can sound like suggestions to be more passive and accepting. Mindfulness and meditation practices ask us to pause, to slow down and reflect. This might make it seem like this book's message is to avoid conflict. It's not. Instead, the last practice, don't wait, is meant to cut through and counterbalance our self-protective tendency to hesitate, minimize, avoid, or assume we have to have everything figured out before acting. Don't wait to find more clarity. Don't wait to practice compassionate accountability. Don't wait to live your life fully.

My good friend Steve, whom I'd known for more than thirty years, was a busy guy with lots of plans. He had just accepted a three-year extension to his role as abbot, or spiritual leader, of the San Francisco Zen Center. It was a demanding position requiring nonstop meetings, lectures, and various interventions and ceremonies around birth, change, and death. Steve had been in this role for seven years, and he looked forward to three more years. His calendar was packed from early morning till evening, and for the next week, months, and even the following year.

> Don't wait to find more clarity. Don't wait to practice compassionate accountability. Don't wait to live your life fully.

One visit to his doctor changed everything. He learned that he had stage-four pancreatic cancer. "What about stage five?" Steve and his wife inquired while sitting with their doctor.

"There is no stage five," the doctor responded.

In an instant, Steve's life changed. His calendar went from being completely full to being completely, starkly empty. It took him several days to process what was happening and to turn himself over to the process of dying.

Steve's story always reminds me that we never know when death will come. We all have plans, but our time here on Earth is short, and it's important to not delay what matters most. This is beautifully captured by a few lines from the poem "Kindness" by Naomi Shihab Nye:

> Before you learn the tender gravity of kindness
> you must travel where the Indian in a white poncho
> lies dead by the side of the road.
> You must see how this could be you,

how he too was someone
who journeyed through the night with plans
and the simple breath that kept him alive.

In the Bible, James 4:14 states this eloquently: "Why, you do not even know what will happen tomorrow. What is your life? You are a mist that appears for a little while and then vanishes."

Renewal, Wholeheartedness, Gratitude

How do we keep ourselves from waiting? How do we make the most of our fleeting time on Earth? How do we stay motivated and keep practicing compassionate accountability, despite all of life's problems, its conflicts and failures, despite all the troubles in society and the world, despite climate change, war, disease, and all the rest?

While it is easy to say and intellectually understand that our lives are short, to live this reality motivates us to find ways to sustain and deepen our sense of security, of belonging, and our ability to open our hearts in the midst of pain and change. That's how we can fully practice what I describe in this book: finding clarity and embodying compassionate accountability. The question is: How do we use the fact that life is short to inspire growth and change and the courage to develop ourselves even in the midst of life's ongoing demands and challenges?

We work hard to learn new practices like compassionate accountability, we notice some growth or change, and then in the next instant, it all seems to fall apart. Perhaps we revert back to old ways of thinking, feeling, and acting. Or instead of responding to a difficult conflict with calm, we become tense and self-critical, or we lash out in frustration, blame, and anger at others. One day we might notice and celebrate our development, our hard-won achievements of greater patience, and then the next day we totally lose our temper during an intense meeting or a heated conversation with a coworker or child. One step forward and two steps back, or so it seems.

Alice, our curiosity expert, knows all about the ever-changing nature of the self:

> "Who are you?" said the Caterpillar....
>
> Alice replied, rather shyly, "I — I hardly know, sir, just at present — at least I know who I was when I got up this morning, but I think I must have been changed several times since then."

Homer, meanwhile, as always, captures our sense of frustration at this:

> I guess some people never change. Or they quickly change and then quickly change back.

We change in countless ways during the course of our lives, depending on the many roles we play and the ways we must face life's myriad challenges. These roles and responsibilities can change from moment to moment: We shift from teacher to learner, from being an individual contributor to team member, from being young to being older. We change jobs and the places we live and find ourselves in new communities. It can be difficult, and at times exasperating, to keep track of all these varying, quickly changing identities and to respond appropriately and well, with our best selves and highest aspirations, staying with what matters most.

Here are three practices that I've found to be helpful: renewal, wholeheartedness, and gratitude.

Renewal: Everywhere You Go Is Your Temple

I once led an all-day silent retreat for a group of a dozen Google engineers. They had previously participated in a series of mindfulness and emotional intelligence workshops that I was developing and teaching at Google headquarters. During these workshops, I had often spoken of the benefits of daylong retreats, and they wanted to experience what it was like to be silent for an entire day.

They were quite a diverse group: twelve men and women ranging in age from twenty-five to fifty-five, with ethnic backgrounds that made the retreat something of a mini–United Nations. Participants hailed from Asia, Europe, South America, Australia, and the United States. We spent the day mostly in silence, which included thirty-minute periods of sitting meditation, several periods of walking meditation indoors and outdoors, and times writing in a journal. We gathered at the end of the day to talk about the experience.

I was surprised to hear how much impact this retreat had. The majority of participants responded by saying something like, "Wow, I had no idea what meditation really was until this day of silence." They experienced a depth of feeling and a sense of connection with themselves and others that was unexpected. They wondered how to sustain and integrate this experience and these feelings into their work and everyday lives. "Do we need to leave our jobs at Google and go to a monastery to continue this kind of practice?" several of them inquired.

This made me smile. "Yes, of course," I responded, "you can leave your jobs, if that is really your path. A monastic experience is terrific, but not practical or accessible for most people. However, nearly everyone can create a monastic-like setting in your home, a sacred spot, a small corner where you can practice meditation regularly."

To foster renewal on an everyday basis, do this. Find a space, or create a space, where you can meditate or write in a journal without being disturbed. If you have children, you might need to practice early, before the daily activity begins. Put some objects there — a stone, a candle, or a word like "breathe," "here," "let it go" — anything that helps remind you to return to your more clear, full-functioning self. Then, try meditating for ten, twenty, or thirty minutes a day, or try journal writing, reading, and reflecting, and see how this influences your work and daily life. Explore bringing the approach of curiosity and spaciousness into your everyday activities.

The point is to let go of the mistaken belief that there are only certain times and ways to practice renewal. Anytime is a good time to find clarity. A powerful way to reset and renew, to sustain and deepen your practice of finding clarity, is to approach all activities — at work and at home, alone and with others — as opportunities for finding clarity.

I've always been drawn to Stephen Covey's metaphor for the importance of resetting and renewal: "sharpening

the saw." Don't wait until the saw is dull.
Regularly sharpen the saw — in part
through meditation and listening to
your heart, by pausing and accessing
your intuitive self — so it never becomes too dull to be effective, to see
clearly, to untangle the tangles. We
are each the saw, and our whetstone
is the realization that life is short, which
helps us to cut through distractions and im-
pediments and take action now to become more clear.

Explore bringing the approach of curiosity and spaciousness into your everyday activities.

Wholeheartedness: The Cure for Exhaustion

Feeling regularly exhausted and depleted can be a sign that
we are out of alignment with what really matters to us. We
become so overwhelmed with the daily demands that it
seems like we have no energy to do anything. However,
poet David Whyte said, "The antidote to exhaustion isn't
rest. The antidote to exhaustion is wholeheartedness."

There are at least two kinds of exhaustion. One kind
is when our intentions, feelings, and activities are not all
in alignment. It's interesting that the word that is trans-
lated as "suffering" in Buddhist texts is the Pali word
dukkha, which literally means "a wheel out of alignment."
A journey with a wheel out of alignment is more difficult,
exhausting, stressful, and unsatisfactory. Stopping and
resting can provide temporary relief, but it doesn't solve
the critical out-of-alignment problem.

The other, more-positive kind of exhaustion is when we
feel well-used, like at the end of a full workday, or after

any activity when we've been fully engaged, where our intentions and actions are mostly aligned. I usually feel great and tired at the end of these days and love the feeling of being "well-spent." It's a good kind of exhaustion.

When exhaustion threatens to undermine your passion, effectiveness, or effort, start by noticing where you might feel out of balance in your work and relationships, or in any part of your life. Then consider how you can find more alignment, greater wholeheartedness, satisfaction, and inspiration. Let yourself feel this deeply, what alignment and lack of alignment feels like. The activity of stopping, sitting, and simply noticing the breath with a sincere effort is itself an activity that generates wholeheartedness. What does it feel like when you bring yourself fully to just being with your body, breath, and feelings? Awareness is the place to begin.

Then, no matter what area or issue feels out of whack, see if you can realign the wheel and engage with more commitment, more wholeheartedness. Reduce any activities where you notice that doing them is depleting you. Consider whether these are activities you should let go of, perhaps completely or indefinitely, or notice if there is a way you are approaching them that you need to change.

The workplace is a useful and important place to practice wholeheartedness. If we're out of alignment at work, this can show up as cynicism, blame, stress, and many other forms of dissatisfaction, which can then bleed into our personal lives. These manifestations can all be signals that we need to engage in our relationship to work to restore a sense of balance and even flow in our life.

The beautiful thing about the practice of wholehearted-ness, like renewal, is that it's always available, everywhere. No need to wait! We can be wholeheartedly grumpy, griev-ing, joyful, bored, or loving. We can be wholeheartedly resistant, afraid, or inspired. When we are wholehearted, we are more present, more alert, and full-functioning — no matter what our state of mind or activity.

Gratitude: Appreciating Your Life

Right now, one highlight of my life is visiting my grandson. As I write these words, he is about to turn three, and just being with my daughter's young son brings me much hap-piness. At the same time, when I'm with him, I can't help but ponder: How much of this person's life will I be alive for? Will I see him enter school? Will I be alive when he becomes a teenager?

Zen teacher Shunryu Suzuki teaches it's the evanes-cence of life that provides meaning and joy. Evanescence is the fleeting, impermanent quality of all things. It's the recognition that life is transitory, that everyone around us will die, and that we will die. This can wake us up to a fresh approach to finding and living with more clarity.

Now is a good time to hug your children, to forgive your parents, to see the awesome beauty of a tree — the awesome beauty of your eyes, heart, and life. Let go of deferring what you were meant to do. Be confident, be humble, be clear, accountable, and compassionate.

Conclusion

Give Me a Lever Long Enough... and I Shall Move the World

Levers are amazing. As I approached my friend to help load a wheelbarrow into the back of his truck, he waved me off and showed me how he could use the edge of his truck's gate as a lever and effortlessly load it himself. It was like magic. Levers make work easier, much easier, by multiplying the effort of the user. Compassionate accountability is a powerful lever.

I think we all have much more influence, potential, and leverage than we usually think. I recently led a compassionate accountability workshop for a group of fifty leaders in the health-care industry. As I was preparing to lead a morning session, the room buzzed with excitement over a magic show everyone had attended the night before.

I was intrigued. The magic show sounded really interesting. Then I began feeling a bit nervous and daunted. How dull would mindfulness and compassionate accountability seem by comparison? My "inner Homer" showed up, and I felt genuinely sorry for myself — just my luck, to have to follow a magic show. What could I possibly do to engage this group of leaders?

Then I surprised myself. I stood up in front of the group to start the session and looked around at the expectant audience.

"I'm a magician, too," I said, and after a suitably dramatic pause, I shared a quote by Vietnamese Zen teacher Thich Nhat Hanh:

> The real miracle isn't to walk on water. The real miracle is to walk right here on Earth.

As I said these words, I felt energized by the magic and the leverage of just being present and alive in that room with a group of curious and open-minded business leaders. It was a simple, ordinary, and profound moment. Just by showing up, with everything I had, I felt the power and presence of my entire life, from my aspiration to help my father to bringing my years of Zen practice into the corporate world. In any moment, perhaps in every moment, we have the ability to transform doubt and fear into possibility, courage, and connection. This transformation might seem magical, but it's simply the result of leveraging each moment we are alive.

Our authentic presence is a potent lever. It can unleash the art and practice of finding clarity and compassionate accountability. It helps us lift the hearts and minds of those we work and live with. It helps us accomplish more with less effort by working together to solve essential problems. The impact of our presence, and the results of our actions, ripple outward like a small pebble reverberating in a still pond.

This book presents a series of mindsets and practices

that, when used skillfully, act like levers that make tremendous change possible:

- Be curious, not furious
- Drop the story
- Listen for understanding
- Mind the gaps
- Cultivate a clear vision
- Turn breakdowns into breakthroughs
- Don't wait

Let's breathe, walk, work, and live together, right here on Earth. Let's cultivate more clarity and compassionate accountability, to support each other, to create thriving work cultures, to solve pressing and essential problems, and to make the impossible possible.

Acknowledgments

Thank you, Lori Hanau of Global Round Table Leadership. Working together, side by side with Lori, Kate McGowan, and the GRTL team was my initiation into embracing the practice of compassionate accountability. Thanks for the inspiration.

To my ZBA and Zen Bones Team: Michelle Keane, Sebastian Mitre, Travis Hellstrom, and Nettie Reynolds, for extraordinary support and creativity.

Thanks to Randell Leach, Angie Podolak, Grant Word, Jennifer Finger, Lawrence Henry, and all the leaders and team members of Beneficial State Bank for exploring and developing the practice of compassionate accountability. I continue to learn from you all.

Kate Sears, who became a core writing and feedback partner as well as Deborah Nelson, Jackie McGrath, and Vanessa Meade.

This book would not have been possible without Jason Gardner of New World Library believing in me.

This book would not be the same without the work of Jeff Campbell's editing touch and magic.

My children, Jason and Carol, for their ongoing, unrestrained critical eye as well as their essential support.

And to my life partner, Lee, for always raising the bar to more awareness and quality, for always showing up new, fresh, and genuine.

Appendix 1

The Heart Sutra

This is my own modern and loose adaptation of the standard English translation of the Heart Sutra, as chanted at the San Francisco Zen Center and numerous Zen practice centers around the world. The Heart Sutra is generally somewhat impenetrable. This version is intended to provide greater accessibility to a wide audience. For further study, see *The Heart of Understanding* by Thich Nhat Hanh.

Why does the Heart Sutra matter? How is the Heart Sutra useful? It is a guide and a practice for not being caught by our assumptions and our stories. It can support us to keep our minds and hearts open, especially during challenging times. It is a way to stay more open, to look more deeply underneath the surface of how we perceive ourselves and the world. It is a way to train the mind to not be limited by our stories, a way to embrace greater appreciation, accountability, and compassion.

Opening Hearts and Minds Sutra

Our everyday view of ourselves is a mirage. See and embody that there is no fixed self, and your life, your suffering, will be transformed.

Everything is not what it seems. Everything is transitory and lacking a subject and an object. What we take for granted as subject and object, as fixed or as form, is lacking, or empty of a fixed self, empty of subject and object.

What we perceive as form does not differ from emptiness. Emptiness does not differ from form. Form itself is emptiness, emptiness itself form. Everything that makes up our sense of self, sensations, perceptions, formations, and consciousness is also like this.

All reality is marked by emptiness; neither arising nor ceasing, neither defiled nor pure, neither increasing nor decreasing.

Therefore, within emptiness, there is no form, no sensation, no perception, no formation, no consciousness; no eyes, no ears, no nose, no tongue, no body, no mind; no sight, no sound, no smell, no taste, no touch, no object of mind; no realm of sight...no realm of mind consciousness. There is neither ignorance nor extinction of ignorance...neither what we think of as old age and death, nor extinction of what we think of as old age and death; no suffering, no cause, no cessation, no path; no knowledge and no attainment.

Nothing is as it seems. Everything is exactly as it seems.

There is nothing to attain. With nothing to attain, rely on the Opening Hearts and Minds Sutra.

When we let go of grasping and aversion, the mind is without hindrance. Without hindrance, there is no fear. Far beyond all grasping and aversion, one realizes freedom. All awakened ones of past, present, and future rely on seeing more clearly, and thereby attain unsurpassed, complete, perfect freedom. This practice removes all suffering and is true, not false.

Open your mind and your heart. Let go. Let everything go. Let go beyond letting go!

Appendix 2

Company Survey

A powerful and effective way to take the pulse of your company or organizational culture is with an anonymous survey. This is an excellent way to gain insights about the gaps in your organization, gaps in the difference between what is and your goals and aspirations for the type of culture you want. With this information you can formulate a development plan that integrates compassionate accountability. Once you have the results, be careful about not overreacting. See any differences between these results and your expectations as gaps. Notice what is working well and what needs attention and improvement. Share the results and begin the work of creating a development plan. Use the gaps and the results and next steps as an opportunity to practice compassionate accountability.

For each statement, ask staff to answer on a scale of 1 to 5: 1 = Agree; 2 = Somewhat agree; 3 = Neutral; 4 = Disagree; 5 = Strongly disagree.

Culture

_____ My efforts to balance my work and personal life are supported.

_____ I fit well in the company culture.

_____ The company is a fun place to work.

_____ The company supports my personal growth and development of emotional intelligence.

_____ The company operates with integrity.

_____ There is a climate of trust within the company.

_____ I would recommend the company as an excellent place to work.

_____ I am excited about the company's future.

_____ I am proud to be a part of the company.

_____ I feel empowered to get things done at the company.

_____ The work environment is open to and helps navigate difficult conversations.

_____ Our team communicates directly around conflicts or challenges.

_____ My work schedule is flexible enough to meet my personal/family needs.

Individual Involvement

_____ My job makes good use of my skills and abilities.

_____ My work gives me a sense of personal accomplishment.

_____ I have sufficient resources to get things done at the company (technology, tools, and so on).

_____ I am appropriately involved in decisions that affect my work.

_____ I am able to follow through on tasks or projects to completion.

_____ I feel motivated to go beyond my formal job requirements to get the job done.

_____ I am sufficiently familiar with company products and offerings to effectively discuss them with people outside of our organization.

_____ I have a clear understanding of what the company's mission and objectives are.

_____ I can see a clear link between my work and the company's objectives. I have a clear understanding of what is expected of me in my job.

_____ I understand how my performance is evaluated.

_____ I know what skills I will need in the future to be a valuable contributor at the company.

_____ When I do an excellent job, my accomplishments are recognized.

Work Group Practices

_____ My work group gets the support it needs from other work groups to achieve our objectives.

_____ My work group has a climate in which diverse perspectives are valued. Problems in my work group are resolved quickly.

_____ My work group looks for ways to change processes to improve productivity.

_____ In my work group, we effectively allocate people/resources based on priorities and skills.

_____ My work group has sufficient resources (e.g., tools, technology, head count) to get the work done.

_____ My work group is able to follow projects through to completion.

_____ Decision-making within my work group is a balance of directive leadership and collaboration.

_____ People in my work group treat each other with respect.

_____ In my work group, we deal effectively with low performers.

Management: Manager

_____ My manager has regular one-on-ones.

_____ My manager understands the challenges of the work.

_____ My manager shows support during challenging times.

_____ My manager is available to me when I have questions or need help.

_____ My manager is open to discussing concerns and complaints.

_____ The actions of my manager show that they value the perspective I bring to the team, even if it is different from their own.

_____ My manager demonstrates comfort with ambiguity/complexity and is able to navigate through it.

_____ My manager is able to initiate and/or engage in difficult conversations.

_____ My manager takes action when important issues are raised from within our work group.

_____ My manager acknowledges successes and contributions of individuals and departments.

_____ My manager regularly shares relevant information from their manager and senior leadership.

_____ My manager communicates a clear sense of direction.

_____ My manager communicates clear goals for the work group.

_____ My manager communicates a clear vision / strategy for the work group.

_____ My manager keeps the work group focused on our priority results / deliverables.

_____ My manager helps me understand how my work impacts the goals of the organization.

_____ My manager gives me regular and actionable feedback to help me improve my performance.

_____ My manager makes it easier for me to get my work done (e.g., follows through, removes roadblocks, gets the resources I need, connects me with the right people).

_____ My manager does not "micromanage" (get involved in details that should be handled at other levels).

_____ My manager works with the group to get the work done when needed.

_____ My manager helps me identify opportunities (e.g., projects, learning programs) to develop my skills and career.

_____ My manager has had a meaningful discussion with me about career development — not just promotions — in the past six months.

_____ My manager models the company's unique culture.

_____ My manager has the technical expertise required to effectively manage me.

_____ Overall, my manager is an effective people manager.

Management: CEO

_____ Our CEO is approachable and available for questions, feedback, or help.

_____ Our CEO is open to discussing concerns and complaints.

_____ Our CEO demonstrates comfort with ambiguity / complexity and is able to navigate through it.

_____ Our CEO is able to initiate and / or engage in difficult conversations.

_____ Our CEO takes action when important issues are raised from within our team.

_____ Our CEO follows through on commitments.

_____ Our CEO acknowledges successes and contributions of individuals and departments.

_____ The actions of my CEO show that they value the perspective I bring to the team, even if it is different from their own.

_____ Decision-making within the organization is a healthy balance of directive leadership from the CEO and input from the team.

_____ Our CEO communicates a clear sense of direction.

_____ Our CEO communicates what is important for our organization to focus on.

_____ Our CEO communicates what is important for each group to focus on to contribute to the company's overall strategy and goals.

_____ Our CEO models the company's unique culture. Overall, our CEO is an effective leader of the organization.

Total Reward / Compensation

_____ I am satisfied with my benefits (e.g., health insurance, retirement / 401(k), vacation / holidays, and so on).

_____ I understand my total compensation package (e.g., salary, health and company benefits).

_____ At the company, people are rewarded according to their job performance.

_____ I am paid fairly for the work I do.

_____ My pay is competitive compared to similar jobs at other companies.

Career Development / Retention

_____ I understand my possible career paths at the company.

_____ The company offers learning resources to help me build my core job-related skills (e.g., coding, sales).

_____ When I am ready to change jobs, there will be good job opportunities for me within the company. I feel that my career goals can be met at the company.

_____ If I were offered a comparable position with similar pay and benefits at another company, I would stay at this company.

_____ I expect to be working at the company one year from now.

_____ I expect to be working at the company five years from now.

_____ At the present time, I am not seriously considering leaving the company.

_____ I understand the criteria I will be evaluated on for promotion.

Appendix 3

Finding Clarity Group Circles

A clarity circle is a group process that emphasizes the practices of deep listening and compassionate accountability to build greater self-awareness, understanding, and effective relationships. This process comes originally from the work of Parker Palmer's *A Hidden Wholeness*. It is a Quaker-based deep-listening methodology.

Groups can meet monthly for an hour or two (or longer), in-person or virtually. The ideal group size is eight to ten people if meeting in person, and five to seven if meeting virtually. It's useful to have one group member act as a moderator to help guide the process and also to track and confirm meeting times.

In addition to group members checking in with one another, the central activity is for one person to present an issue, a problem, something in their work or life where they need more clarity. They might need more clarity during an important transition or about a work or family relationship.

Part 1: Checking In

Each person has five minutes (or more) to address personal, family, and/or work topics. What's going well? What needs improvement? What are you looking forward to? What are you not looking forward to?

Give members a few minutes to write down their thoughts. Each person might fill out a grid like the one below. Then each person shares and expands upon what they write. If time allows, you can also create space for questions or comments after each person reports.

	Going well	Not going well	Looking forward to	Not looking forward to
Personal				
Family				
Work				

Part 2: Clarity Circle

Following the check-ins, transition to the clarity circle.

A clarity circle is a process for finding clarity through deep listening and inquiry. One person presents an issue in their work or life where they need more clarity. The group members listen and ask clarifying questions. The process aims to mine the wisdom of the group through curiosity and openness instead of advice-giving.

Here is one way to run the process, which you can modify as you wish:

Decide Who Will Present

1. Each person writes down three issues they might present, then they choose one.
2. In less than one minute, each person names their issue to present.
3. The group decides who will present, based on which issue has the most need and is an issue that the group feels it can effectively engage with.

Presentation

1. The presenter has seven minutes, uninterrupted, to describe the issue. What are they looking for and not looking for? Describe where more clarity is needed.
2. Then, group members are given twelve minutes to ask clarifying questions. The presenter responds to each question. No advice-giving.
3. One minute of silence.
4. Each person has one minute to name an

experience they had that was similar, starting with "This reminds me of..."

5. One minute of silence.

6. The presenter describes what they are taking away from this process.

Closing

1. Each person says two words that summarize what they are taking from the process or what they are feeling right now.

At the end of each group meeting, you can decide who will present an issue to the group at the following meeting.

Endnotes

p. vii   *Will you ever bring a better gift for the world*: William Stafford, *The Way It Is* (Minneapolis, MN: Graywolf Press, 1999).

Introduction

p. 8   *In a recent survey, Gallup found*: Jon Clifton, "The World's Workplace Is Broken — Here's How to Fix It," Gallup, June 14, 2022, https://www.gallup.com/work place/393395/world-workplace-broken-fix.aspx.

p. 8   *From 2020 to 2021, employee engagement declined*: Jim Harter, "U.S. Employee Engagement Slump Contin-ues," Gallup, April 25, 2022, https://www.gallup .com/workplace/391922/employee-engagement -slump-continues.aspx.

p. 8   *US employees spend approximately 2.8 hours*: CPP Global Human Capital Report, "Workplace Conflict and How Businesses Can Harness It to Thrive," July 2008.

p. 8   *In the United States, 60 percent of employees*: Pol-lack Peacebuilding Systems, "Workplace Conflict

Statistics: Updated 2020," accessed November 2, 2022, https://pollackpeacebuilding.com/workplace-conflict-statistics.

p. 8   *On average, companies with a healthy corporate culture*: Pollack Peacebuilding Systems, "Workplace Conflict Statistics."

p. 8   *A 2021 UK study reported that 485,800 UK employees*: Richard Saundry and Peter Urwin, "Estimating the Costs of Workplace Conflict," Acas, May 11, 2021, https://www.acas.org.uk/estimating-the-costs-of-workplace-conflict-report.

p. 9   *In our families, on average, 27 percent*: Karl Pillemer, *Fault Lines* (New York: Avery, 2020).

p. 9   *Poet David Whyte was once leading a public reading*: Lisa Burrell, "A Larger Language for Business," *Harvard Business Review*, May 2007, https://hbr.org/2007/05/a-larger-language-for-business.

p. 10   *The man was a senior leader at Boeing*: David Whyte, *Clear Mind, Wild Heart* (Louisville, CO: Sounds True, 2002).

p. 10   *Today, it takes as many as six thousand suppliers*: Faye Bowers, "Building a 747: 43 Days and 3 Million Fasteners," *Christian Science Monitor*, October 29, 1997, https://www.csmonitor.com/1997/1029/102997.us.us.2.html.

p. 11   *"the gold standard of American industry"*: Charles Bramesco, "'All Those Agencies Failed Us': Inside the Terrifying Downfall of Boeing," *Guardian*, February 22, 2022, https://www.theguardian.com/film/2022/feb/22/downfall-the-case-against-boeing-netflix-documentary-737-max.

p. 11   *The 2022 documentary* Downfall: *Downfall: The Case Against Boeing*, directed by Rory Kennedy (Beverly Hills, CA: Imagine Documentaries, 2022), Netflix, https://www.netflix.com/title/81272421.

p. 11   *"There were many decades when Boeing did"*: Bramesco, "'All Those Agencies Failed Us.'"

p. 11   *In 2021 Boeing was fined $2.5 billion by the US Justice Department*: Niraj Chokshi and Michael Schmidt, "Boeing Reaches $2.5 Billion Settlement with U.S. Over 737 Max," *New York Times*, January 7, 2021, https://www.nytimes.com/2021/01/07/business/boeing-settlement-justice-department.html.

Chapter 1: Be Curious, Not Furious

p. 24   *Apparently, the expression "curiosity killed the cat"*: This expression originates from the 1598 play by English playwright Ben Jonson, *Every Man in His Humour*: "Helter skelter, hang sorrow, care'll kill a Cat, up-tails all, and a Louse for the Hangman."

p. 36   *The "Stretch Zone Chart"*: The Stretch Zone chart was adapted from the original version created by Ute Limacher-Riebold, PhD, https://utesinternational lounge.com.

p. 39   *In a 2005 study, psychologists Kevin Ochsner and James Gross*: Kevin Ochsner and James Gross, "The Cognitive Control of Emotion," *Trends in Cognitive Sciences* 9, no. 5 (May 2005): 242–49, https://www.science direct.com/science/article/abs/pii/S136466130 5000902.

Chapter 2: Drop the Story

p. 46   *"All experience is preceded by mind"*: Gil Fronsdal, trans., *The Dhammapada* (Boston: Shambhala, 2005).

p. 48   *Psychologist and leading organizational development pioneer Chris Argyris*: Peter Senge, *The Fifth Discipline* (New York: Currency/Doubleday, 2006).

p. 56   *He wrote, "With each exhale, let go of everything"*: Shunryu Suzuki, *Not Always So* (New York: Harper-Collins, 2002).

Chapter 3: Listen for Understanding

p. 74   *"I cannot experience your experience"*: R.D. Lang, The Politics of Experience (New York: Pantheon Books, 1969).

p. 77   *"Who is this miracle speaking to me?"*: Marilyn Nelson, "Generous Listening," On Being Gathering, April 11, 2018, https://onbeing.org/poetry/generous-listening.

Chapter 5: Cultivate a Clear Vision

p. 120   *Seek to embody the classic text by Lao-tzu*: Stephen Mitchell, trans., *Tao Te Ching* (New York: Harper-Collins, 2006).

Chapter 6: Turn Breakdowns into Breakthroughs

p. 127   *"The ground where you stumble"*: Suzuki, *Not Always So.*

p. 132   *First introduced at Harvard by Amy Edmondson*: Amy Edmondson, *The Fearless Organization* (Hoboken, NJ: John Wiley & Sons, 2019).

p. 132 *a study that was conducted by Google*: "Guide: Understand Team Effectiveness," Google, re:Work, accessed November 7, 2022, https://rework.withgoogle .com/print/guides/5721312655835136.

p. 135 *In* The Splendid and the Vile, *author Erik Larson*: Erik Larson, *The Splendid and the Vile* (New York: Crown, 2020).

p. 143 *"Last night as I was sleeping"*: Antonio Machado, *Selected Poems,* trans. Alan Trueblood (Boston: Harvard University Press, 1988).

Chapter 7: Don't Wait

p. 145 *"When it's over, I want to say"*: Mary Oliver, "When Death Comes," *New and Selected Poems* (1992; repr., Boston: Beacon Press, 2007).

p. 146 *"Before you learn the tender gravity of kindness"*: Naomi Shihab Nye, "Kindness," *Different Ways to Pray* (Portland, OR: Breitenbush Publications, 1980).

About the Author

M arc Lesser is a CEO, executive coach, trainer, and Zen teacher with more than twenty-five years of experience as a leader supporting leaders to reach their full potential, as business executives and as full, thriving human beings. He is currently CEO of ZBA Associates, an executive coaching and development organization.

Marc helped develop the world-renowned Search Inside Yourself program within Google. He cofounded and was CEO of the Search Inside Yourself Leadership Institute. Marc was tapped for this role based on having been CEO of three companies, having an MBA degree from New York University, and having sat more than ten thousand hours of mindfulness meditation.

Marc has coached executives and led trainings in Fortune 500 companies, start-ups, health care, and government. He has trained hundreds of teachers worldwide as mindfulness and emotional intelligence trainers.

Marc is the author of four previous books, including *Seven Practices of a Mindful Leader: Lessons from Google and a Zen Monastery Kitchen* and *Less: Accomplishing More by Doing Less.*

Prior to his business and coaching career, Marc was a resident of the San Francisco Zen Center for ten years, including one year as director of Tassajara Zen Mountain Center, the first Zen monastery in the Western world. He has a passion for utilizing business as a force for positive change and sees work as a place to cultivate character and bring meaning and satisfaction to everyday life.

In 2022, Marc launched the podcast *Zen Bones: Ancient Wisdom for Modern Times* (marclesser.net/podcast). It features interviews with the world's leading thinkers and activists, as well as mindfulness practice sessions.

For more, visit marclesser.net and the Zen Bones Substack newsletter at marclesser.substack.com.

NEW WORLD LIBRARY is dedicated to publishing books and other media that inspire and challenge us to improve the quality of our lives and the world.

We are a socially and environmentally aware company. We recognize that we have an ethical responsibility to our readers, our authors, our staff members, and our planet.

We serve our readers by creating the finest publications possible on personal growth, creativity, spirituality, wellness, and other areas of emerging importance. We serve our authors by working with them to produce and promote quality books that reach a wide audience. We serve New World Library employees with generous benefits, significant profit sharing, and constant encouragement to pursue their most expansive dreams.

Whenever possible, we print our books with soy-based ink on 100 percent postconsumer-waste recycled paper. We power our offices with solar energy and contribute to nonprofit organizations working to make the world a better place for us all.

Our products are available wherever books are sold. Visit our website to download our catalog, subscribe to our e-newsletter, read our blog, and link to authors' websites, videos, and podcasts.

customerservice@newworldlibrary.com
Phone: 415-884-2100 or 800-972-6657
Orders: Ext. 110 • Catalog requests: Ext. 110
Fax: 415-884-2199

newworldlibrary.com